It Took a War

IT TOOK A WAR

EMILY ANN PUTZKE

The
White
Rose
Press

ISBN 978-0692341391

Published by The White Rose Press

This novel is a work of fiction. Though actual locations may be mentioned, they are used in a fictitious manner and the events and occurrences were invented in the mind and imagination of the author. Similarities of characters to any person, past, present, or future, are coincidental.

Images on cover obtained from
http://www.loc.gov/pictures/resource/ppmsca.34967/,

http://www.loc.gov/pictures/resource/ppmsca.34360/ and

Shuttershock.com

Cover design and interior layout:

Rachel Rossano of Rossano Designs
(RossanoDesigns.weebly.com)

Print Edition

To:

Mom and dad, for your never ending love and support. Thank you for everything!

"It is history that teaches us to hope."

-Robert E. Lee

Chapter One

1861

It was one of those crisp April mornings when the world smelled sweet and fresh, as if it had just been thoroughly cleansed. Joe Roberts sat on the bottom porch step as he munched on a piece of bread with jam that he had snatched from the kitchen moments before. He stared at the Pennsylvania mountains that surrounded him on every side as they sliced through the thick morning fog. They made him anxious.

Prison walls. Those mountains ain't nothin' but prison walls.

He looked over his shoulder as the front door opened and was relieved to see it was only his sisters, Coralie and Isabelle, and not his roguish cousin, Lucas. Mama told him that Lucas was to be referred to as his brother. He was, after all, an official part of the family since Uncle Simeon died. But Joe couldn't bring himself to confessing any sort of kinship with Lucas.

I won't ever call him my brother. I'd die first.

"Mornin'," he mumbled to the girls, scooting over to allow them room to sit.

Coralie sat down with a friendly, "Good morning, Joe," while four year old Isabelle scrambled onto Joe's lap and snuggled into his chest.

"What time is it?" he asked Coralie.

"Almost seven," she said. "But Izzy's been awake since five and I had a time of it, trying to keep her quiet. She started singing and Lucas heard her from across the hall. He got flaming mad, pounded on our door and yelled at the top of his lungs. He's not very agreeable this morning."

"Is he ever agreeable?" Joe held on tightly to Isabelle who was hugging his arms around herself and humming a song.

"What are we going to do today? It's a fine morning, don't you think?" Coralie said, her brown eyes looking bright and cheerful in the morning light.

"Why don't we go fishin' and wade in the creek?" Joe suggested.

Coralie's eyes widened and she shook her head quickly, her braids whipping against her cheeks. "Mama would be horrified! It's not proper for a young lady to fish, Joe!"

Joe couldn't help but snicker at that. "Hogwash, Coralie. What ain't proper about fishin'?"

"I could name quite a few things," said Coralie, sticking her chin in the air as she smoothed the wrinkles from her dress.

"You ever been fishin'?" Joe asked, looking over Isabelle's curly head to peer at Coralie.

"No."

"I haven't either!" Isabelle whirled around and stared up at Joe, excitement flashing in her deep blue eyes.

"Well, come on little sisters. It's time you learned." Joe stood up as Isabelle crawled off his lap. She jumped down the steps, her messy braids flying about, and grabbed his hand. Her's was hot and sticky, and Joe grimaced as he realized that Isabelle hadn't washed after breakfast. Coralie, however, didn't budge from her spot on the porch, but Joe was determined to take her along on their expedition, "Aw, come on, Coralie. It'll be a lark."

Coralie, try as she might to be a proper young lady, was apt to enjoy adventures over sitting and doing needlework, which was what she would be doing this morning if she didn't join the frolic. She rolled her eyes, "Oh, all right. It does sound like fun, even if it *is* a little boyish."

"Let's hurry then!" Joe and Isabelle scampered down the road past the modest neighboring houses which were encircled by white picket fences. Their neighbors' gardens were blooming, sending off sweet scents, and the brick walkways leading to their doors were wet from the morning dew. They strolled by the general store, and Joe couldn't help but grimace. The sign above the door was

3

starting to slip, and Joe knew that Mama would be after him about fixing it. The O and R in *Roberts* were faded, and the edges of the sign that once had been white were now an unattractive grey.

He picked up his pace and ran down the road with Isabelle in tow, shrieking in laughter as the cool wind whipped against their faces. When he glanced back, Coralie seemed to be deciding whether to walk like a lady or run ahead with him. Joe smiled as she finally broke into a sprint toward him. "Coralie! Young ladies *don't* run!" he teased.

The trio darted into the edge of the woods and slipped through the dense leaves and bushes. Twigs snapped under their boots and branches poked out to block their way. The scent of damp earth smelled good and Joe felt certain that this was much better than working in the blasted store, running deliveries, or being plagued by his cousin. In fact, if he had his way, he would never return. He would live in the woods and fish all day long.

"Did you bring your pocketknife, Joe?" Coralie suddenly asked him as she clung to his sleeve. Her fingernails dug into his arm, and he cringed from the pain.

"Sure I did. But what will I be needin' it for?"

She took a shaky breath, "Are there bears or coyotes in these woods?"

Now Isabelle started whining and squeezed his hand. Joe grinned wickedly. "Well, of course. They're all over the place. You best be careful and stay right close to me or…what was that sound? Did you hear that? Where's my pocket knife?" He let go of Isabelle's sticky hand and pried Coralie's nails out of his skin, then pretended to search for his pocketknife.

Coralie scanned the woods as her face drained of color, and her eyes grew large with fear. Isabelle was clinging to Coralie now, and the sisters stood there whimpering. They were so wrapped up in their momentary concern that they didn't notice Joe circling behind them. He made growling noises deep in his throat as he picked up a pebble from the ground and tossed it into the edge of the woods to imitate the sound of an animal pursuer. The girls jumped and let out a high pitched cry that rang in Joe's ears and made him howl in laughter.

Coralie whirled around and slapped Joe's face hard. It stung, and he immediately caressed the side of his face with his hand to soothe it. Coralie's eyes were huge, and her bottom lip quivered as she scrunched up her nose and pouted, "You're just about the meanest person I know! I'm going home. Take us home, Joe." Coralie started to take a step but Joe caught her arm.

"I was only teasin'. You're safe with me. No bears or coyotes are gonna get you."

Coralie narrowed her eyes at him, one hand holding Isabelle's wrist and the other pointed at Joe. "You, *promise?*"

Joe nodded and was surprised that she seemed to believe him, as she grabbed his sleeve again. Isabelle wanted him to hold her, so he scooped her up, and she clung to his neck, her warm face pressed against his. The woods were quiet now except for the crunching of their feet on leaves and the occasional chirping of birds. They soon approached a stream of water, and it was so pure that you could see right to the bottom. Water spiders strided along the surface, leaving rings in their wake.

Isabelle wriggled out of Joe's arms, ran over to the water and started chattering about the spiders. Joe, meanwhile, headed for the hollow tree that homed his fishing pole and a jar of plump worms. He settled himself on a large, cold rock and pulled off his shoes. Coralie sat next to him and watched as he hooked a fat worm.

"That's horrible!" Coralie turned her face away and covered it with her hands.

"No it ain't. See here, Coralie, if you want to learn how to fish, you need to learn how to put bait on the hook. Otherwise you won't catch nothin'."

"I never said I wanted to learn how to fish."

"As your big brother I feel it my duty to teach you. Now turn around and watch. Izzy, get away from the water. You'll scare all the fish away."

Coralie and Isabelle watched as Joe casted a line into the water. A long moment passed as they stared at the slow water sliding over the rocks.

"Ain't something supposed to happen?" Coralie looked from the water to Joe in curiosity.

"Don't say *ain't*, Coralie. It ain't proper."

Coralie's mouth fell open and she pointed at him, "You say it all the time! Why can't I?"

"'Cause you're a young lady, remember? You're suppose to talk all fancy like." Joe gave a slight tug on the line, then settled back with the pole between his legs and pushed his cap over his eyes. The sunlight laced through the trees and warmed his face, perfect for a morning doze.

"Why are you leaning back? What if you catch something? Won't it pull you down?" Isabelle wanted to know as she tugged on Joe's arm.

Joe glanced at his naive little sister from under his cap and shook his head with a little laugh. "There ain't fish *that* big in this creek, Izzy. Besides, I'm always ready."

Coralie and Isabelle leaned back on their hands, crossed their ankles and waited for something to happen. The lull of the quiet water mixed with the wind swirling through the trees took Joe away into a nice, relaxing sleep. That is, until Coralie's scream bolted him awake. Joe's eyes flew open as his fishing pole started to slide down the rock. Quickly, he grabbed at it and tried pulling it up, but his foot slid down the rock, causing him to tumble into the creek. He lost his grip on the pole as frigid water stung his eyes, nose and filled his mouth, making it nearly impossible to breath.

Joe wrestled with the water until finally he came to the surface, gasping for breath. His limbs felt frozen to his side. Coralie was standing on the shore with a long stick in her hand and yelling at the top of her lungs, "Joe! Joe! Joe! Oh, Joe! Are you okay, Joe?"

She sure knows how to overuse a person's name.

He stood up, revealing that the water only came to his waist. The coldness had surprised him, but Joe knew that he wasn't going to drown. He pushed his way through the creek to reach the shore and was greeted by Coralie throwing her arms around his wet body and Isabelle looking on with eyes wide as the sky itself. "For goodness sake, girls, don't get so shook up about it."

"But I thought the water was going to take you away, and you would drown! You scared me half to death." Coralie pulled away, her dress now wet and muddy.

"What about the fish? Did you catch it?" Isabelle asked.

He had to smile. It didn't appear that Isabelle was that worried about *him* after all. "No, Izzy, I didn't."

"Well," said Coralie. "I never wanted to go fishing in the first place. Fishing—"

"Ain't for proper young ladies," Joe finished her sentence, leading the way through the woods as his pants clung to his legs, and his shirt felt like a load of bricks.

When they reached home, Mama was leaning against the railing of the porch, arms folded and scanning the land with her dark blue eyes. Lucas was sprawling on the porch step with his nose in the paper and glanced up when Joe and his sisters appeared from the woods.

"Mornin'," Joe greeted them as he took off his cap. A puddle of water fell to his feet.

"Where have you been?" Mama demanded. Mama was very short and thin, so when Joe approached, he towered over her.

"I just took Coralie and Izzy down to the creek for a fishin' lesson. I kinda fell in the water is all." Joe stood there, hands behind back and water dripping down his face.

"Joe, you were supposed to be here to open the store this morning. I count on you and Lucas to help me, but you are both in your own little worlds lately. Here you are, soaked to the bone and romping in the woods, and Lucas *won't* work, or so he tells me."

"Well, why can't you work, Lucas? You're just sittin' there readin' the paper," Joe growled.

Lucas' head shot up. His mop of brown hair fell over his forehead, and he glared darkly at Joe, "It ain't my store. I didn't ask to be adopted into this family or to work in *your* store, so why should I?" He stood up, dropped the paper and stalked into the house, slamming the door as he went.

9

Mama cleared her throat and when Joe turned around, he caught her looking into the sky, her face contorted in pain. "Mama, are you all right?" Joe set a hand on her slim shoulder. "Don't cry, Mama."

A single tear ran down her cheek, and she wiped it away with the corner of her apron. Regaining her composure, she smiled at Joe and patted his hand tenderly. "I'm fine, son. Really, I am." She took a deep breath. "Girls, please go inside." Joe watched as his sisters slipped into the house quietly, then turned to face Mama who was staring at him. "There's very important news in the paper today, Joe." She leaned over and carefully picked up the newspaper that Lucas had cast aside. She handed it to Joe, and the first words he caught were:

BY TELEGRAPH:

NEWS FROM CHARLESTON HARBOR,
SOUTH CAROLINA.
WAR! WAR!! WAR!!!

The newspaper waved as a gust of wind came, and Joe gripped it tighter as his eyes darted over the page.

THE REBELS OPEN FIRE ON FORT SUMTER.

THE FIRE RETURNED!

FORT SUMTER SURRENDERS.

WHOLE COUNTRY AROUSED.

GREAT PREPARATIONS FOR WAR.

SEVENTY-FIVE THOUSAND TROOPS
   CALLED FOR BY PRESIDENT.

Joe's eyes lifted and locked with Mama's. "There's to be a real war?" he whistled, then threw the paper in the air exclaiming, "A real live war!"

He received a chiding look in response. "Joe, war is nothing to be excited about."

"I think it is, Mama! The southern states are uprisin' against the Union, and we're gonna squash them! We'll put them back in their place with a real live *war*!" Joe hooted and hollered.

Mama's eyes reflected concern as she picked up the newspaper that had been thrown in Joe's exuberance. "You are not included in that 'we' you speak of, Joe. You're only sixteen. Now, please go open the store."

Joe's patriotic heart shriveled at Mama's words. He glared at the store across the road that would be brimming with customers soon enough.

I hate it. I hate workin' at the store.

He was determined to be among the seventy-five thousand called to end the Southern rebellion.

Joe was going to have himself an adventure.

Chapter Two

"Never do a wrong thing to make a friend or to keep one."
– Robert E. Lee

In my own little world, eh, Aunt Genevieve? Well, it's better than being in your's. I didn't ask for this life!

Lucas kicked the leg of his desk hard and regretted it immediately. Pain shot up and down his leg. He was tempted to curse, but stopped himself as his eyes fell on a daguerreotype laying amidst papers and books on his nightstand. He reached for the photograph, staring at the narrow face of his father, the sweet and tender countenance of his mother, and a young boy he no longer recognized. It was him at the age of three, fifteen years ago. As he stared at the boy, anger brewed inside him. He threw the daguerreotype on the floor in disgust, shards of glass sliding across the floor.

Lucas stared out the window as memories caught up with him.

Will this never leave me?

His mother's face flashed before him, and he could almost feel her tender kiss on his cheek. He remembered Aunt Genevieve weeping when she told him that his mother had died. He didn't remember the words she had said, but he vividly recalled how they felt. Lucas turned his face from the window and paced the floor.

Blast!

He pushed the daguerreotype aside with his foot before throwing open the door and heading for the store.

Fine, Aunt Genevieve. I'll work in the store today – but only as a distraction.

Joe was behind the counter, glaring at Lucas as he walked in the store. "It's about time you got here. I have a delivery to make, so you need to look after the store." Joe grabbed the paperbag from the counter and trudged past Lucas, knocking his shoulder into him. "Oh, and be nice to the customers would you, Lucas? You've scared away more than a few young ladies and little children."

Lucas sent a dark look at his cousin as the door closed behind him. He loathed the store. He loathed dusting the shelves and hauling sacks of flour, sugar, and cornmeal. He loathed working with customers, and he loathed admitting to himself that Joe was right. He did scare away more than a few people. With a heavy sigh, he walked behind the counter and took a seat, swiping a piece of licorice from the glass candy jar. From where he was sitting he could see that the shelves needed a good dusting, the hardwood floor needed sweeping, and the windows were smudged.

I don't care. It ain't my store.

The front door opened, and he quickly stuffed the licorice in his pocket. If it was Aunt Genevieve, she'd make him pay for it. But it was only his young cousin, Isabelle. Lucas would never admit it to anyone, but he thought Isabelle was a sweet little girl. She was full of

14

wonder and joy, most of the time, and her smile was accented with one big dimple on the left cheek. He pulled the licorice out again and continued chewing as he watched her. "What do you want?"

Isabelle folded her chubby arms and marched to the front of the store with a scowl on her rosy face. "You can't eat that licorice, Lucas! Mama says we can't unless we have money to pay for it."

Lucas popped the last of it into his mouth with a smug look on his face. "Well, I just did. What do you want anyhow?"

Isabelle looked around the store then bolted for the corner where a wooden stool held her precious treasure. "I left my doll, Jenny, here yesterday, and I don't want anyone to buy her." Lucas watched as she picked up the rag doll tenderly and kissed its face. "Isn't she pretty?" Isabelle skipped over to the counter and held the doll out for Lucas to see.

Nope. It's ugly, was what Lucas wanted to say.

The doll was hideous with its cone shaped head, five strands of red yarn for hair, two different sized button eyes and a stained white dress that hung off its shoulders.

"Why don't you ask your mother for a nice porcelain doll, like the ones for sale here?" he asked.

Isabelle turned behind her where three porcelain dolls with glossy curls and lace trimmed dresses were displayed. "But none of them are Jenny."

15

Lucas rolled his eyes and snatched another piece of licorice. "You have your doll, now go on home."

"Oh, fine," Isabelle turned. "Coralie is watching me from the house, and she said not to stay long because you're mean." Isabelle skipped out the door, leaving Lucas in the empty store with his thoughts.

Of course Coralie would say that. She hates me.

Time passed slowly as Lucas waited for customers, and his mind started drifting. He tried not to think about the past. He tried to just sit and gaze out the window, but the street was quiet except for the occasional carriage or walking couple. Lately, his mind had been drifting to memories from not so long ago. His memory of the night that changed everything was cloudy. He had been drinking, he knew that. Had too many drinks and slugged someone, and they slugged him back. *Hard.* Lucas could still recall the taste of blood, the whistling of the night wind, the darkness and loneliness of those back streets. Then Joe's father, Uncle Charles, came.

The memories wouldn't go away, and if he kept thinking, they would only get worse. His eyes flew to the door as it cracked open, and he was grateful for a diversion. A group of boys from town stormed in. Lucas knew them. He knew they were thieves and liars, yet those were exactly the friends he seemed to make wherever he went. The tall boy with a mop of blonde hair and grey eyes was Jake, followed by two brothers – Edmund and Richard.

"Got anything good to eat here?" Jake said, swaggering across the store and leaning against the counter.

Lucas opened the top of another candy jar that held spice drops. "Help yourself."

Jake grabbed a fistful of candy and stuck them in his pocket, then grabbed another and stuffed them in his mouth, resembling a chipmunk when he chewed. Edmund and Richard were lurking around the store, and Lucas had a hunch that they were stealing. He peered around Jake's head, spotted Richard snatching a pocket watch and an expensive pair of boots while Edmund slipped two pocket knives into his trousers.

"You figure on payin' for that today?" Lucas asked lazily.

"Why?" Richard asked. "You gonna turn us in? You know that you can't be one of us no more if you do that, and you know what *that* means, don't you, Lucas Holmes?"

Lucas stood up and pushed the candy closer to his friends. "I was pullin' your leg. Take what you want. I don't care. It ain't my store."

Jake glanced over at the cash register with a sly grin. "How much money you got in there?"

Lucas pulled open the register and hesitated only a moment before discreetly stuffing most of the money in his pocket. "Only a couple dollars," he lied as he handed the rest to Jake.

17

"Guess that'll do," Jake replied. He helped himself to another fistful of candy, then turned to Lucas, "Well, I reckon you heard that war's been declared, but did you know about the war rally?"

Lucas was on his fifth piece of licorice and shook his head. "War rally?"

"It's gonna be right in the middle of town. Some man's forming a company and needs boys to enlist."

Lucas' heart sped up. Maybe that was the answer to his problems. He could join the army to escape not only the store, his aunt and cousins, but maybe even those hateful memories of his past. "Are you boys gonna enlist?"

Jake cocked an eyebrow. "Join? Heck no! There will be a crowd of people there, Holmes. A prime place to pick a pocket and get some cash."

Pickin' pockets?

Lucas couldn't help but feel disappointed. "Yeah, I'm sure there will be lots of politicians with loads of money there," he said half-heartedly.

"So, are you gonna join us?" Jake was staring him down.

Lucas shrugged as he put his booted feet on the counter. He considered it and came to the conclusion that he could join his friends, get a little cash, then slip away from them, join the army and be off before anyone noticed or cared. "Sure. When is it?"

"Tomorrow at ten. Meet us outside the town hall."

Lucas nodded as the boys left the store. "Tomorrow. I'll be there."

Chapter Three

"A house divided against itself cannot stand. I believe this government cannot endure permanently half slave and half free. I do not expect the Union to be dissolved; I do not expect the house to fall; but I do expect that it will cease to be divided. It will become all the one thing or all the other."
– Abraham Lincoln

Joe walked along the the long dirt road back to the store, lost in thought. He had been making a delivery to a neighbor, Mrs. Elliott, and as he was placing the paper bag on her kitchen table, he noticed a pile of posters proclaiming the words "War Rally at Town Square" in big black letters. Mrs. Elliott had spotted him looking at it and handed him one eagerly. "My husband and sons have been putting these signs up around town, but we have so many extras. Perhaps you could put one in your store, Joseph?"

Joe had said yes, and here he was, clutching the poster in his hands with a thudding heart at the thought of war. The sight of the store standing against the green mountains didn't appeal to him. He wanted an adventure, but getting Mama to agree with his wish to enlist wouldn't be easy, and he knew it. With a heavy sigh, Joe pushed opened the store door and caught Lucas just as he was putting a handful of spice drops in his mouth.

"You better have money to pay for that," Joe mumbled as he shuffled to the front window. He positioned the poster in the right corner and started tucking it into the edges of the window frame.

"What's that?" Lucas asked.

Joe gritted his teeth. "A war rally sign. But I don't know if Mama will approve of it in the window." He thought a moment and decided that he should confront Mama first, so he tore it down.

"Don't bother puttin' that in the window. There ain't a soul around here who would enlist."

Joe clenched his fists and turned toward Lucas who was helping himself to more candy. He yanked the jar from Lucas and clamped the lid shut. "What do you mean by that? There's plenty of brave men around here."

Lucas snickered and kicked up his feet, his boots sending dirt across the counter. "And I suppose you count yourself one of them?"

Joe didn't know where Lucas was going with this talk but he nodded his head. "I'm a heap braver than you."

"Really?" Lucas' face twisted into a smirk. "You do remember your first huntin' trip, don't you?"

Joe pushed away from the counter. "That's got *nothin'* to do with this." An unwelcome image of black woods surrounded him. He was eleven then, and he'd somehow gotten separated from his father and Lucas. He couldn't find his way home. He'd spent the whole night listening to the eerie sounds of darkness.

"I'm only pointin' out that before you go off and fight in a war, make sure that you ain't scared of the dark no more," Lucas' eyes flashed with amusement.

"I was only a boy, Lucas. It's nothin' to be ashamed of. Not like the things *you* have to live with."

"Your father didn't have to come find me. I was fine on my own. It ain't my fault," Lucas turned his head to the window, and his face suddenly turned stoic.

"If I had my way, Lucas, I'd have thrown you out of the house years ago," Joe spat heartlessly.

"If I had my way, little cousin, I'd never have spent a wakin' moment livin' with you or your family."

"Good. Now we have it out in the open. We despise each other." Joe grabbed the inventory list off the counter and headed over to the shelves. When he approached the clothing and shoe shelf, he noticed that the new pair of boots that had arrived only yesterday were gone.

"Someone bought those boots?" he asked suspiciously. "Mama wasn't sure they would sell. They were expensive and she was angry that I ordered them at all. Who bought them?"

Lucas didn't answer, and he closed his eyes, completely ignoring Joe's question.

"Fine. If you're gonna ignore me, I'll just have a look in the register and make sure the money made it in there." Joe shoved Lucas' feet off the table and leaned over to open the register. His skin went cold. "Where's the money, Lucas?"

23

Lucas sighed and tossed him an indignant look. "I bundled it up and gave it to your mother. If you don't believe me, go ask her."

Joe slammed the register shut and kept his eyes fixed on Lucas. "I think I will."

"No, Lucas didn't give me any money," Mama said. She smelled of yeast and oil, as she had just finished kneading a loaf of bread. She wiped her hands on her starched white apron and cocked her head at Joe. "Why do you ask?"

Joe glanced out the kitchen window, and his breath caught in his throat. The store door was wide open and blowing in the wind.

I'm such a fool! Of course Lucas would run!

Joe's mind whirled, and he could have kicked himself for being so stupid.

Mama covered the gooey dough with a damp cloth and kept looking at Joe out of the corner of her eye. "Joe, please tell me what's going on."

"We have a thief on our hands," Joe called as he ran from the kitchen. He dashed across the street and burst into the store. It was empty. Lucas had made his getaway, leaving behind a trail of dusty boot prints on the floor.

Joe groaned before whipping around and heading back into the road, running a hand through his curly hair.

He's gonna pay for this.

He ran as hard as his legs would allow, weaving past neighbors who were taking a leisurely stroll. "Excuse me! Pardon me! I'm so sorry!" was his constant refrain.

Joe finally stopped and tried to catch his breath. His chest burned from the sudden exertion.

He's gone. Should have known he couldn't stop being such a devil. Blast!

Joe's head ached as he continued the search for his cousin.

Lucas grinned to himself as he crouched behind one of the many oak trees lining the road. Joe ran right past him without noticing. Lucas patted the wad of money in his pocket with satisfaction. The only thing he regretted was not thinking to pack his belongings. Now he would have to slip back into the house and grab his things. Once that task was done, he'd get along just fine, for the army was calling him. He would be far away from his relatives who knew nothing about his plan.

Joe wouldn't enlist. He's too young and wouldn't dare leave his family.

He sat there a moment and watched as Joe kicked a stone with all his might, mumbling under his breath something about a lousy, no good fellow named Lucas. Then Joe hiked back up the road, slipped into the store and slammed the door behind him. Lucas turned to peer at the porch where Isabelle was playing with dolls and Coralie sat in a chair, stitching. Aunt Genevieve was hurrying across the street to the store with an anxious look on her face as the hem of her apron fluttered in the breeze.

Lucas stood up and softly trotted through the woods until he was further down the road, then crossed without a soul noticing. The house was a far distance away, but using the back of the neighbors' homes as a shield, he was able to run quickly across lawns and arrive at the back door of his aunt's white house.

He pushed the door open quietly and darted up the stairs, gaining his bedroom in less than a minute. It didn't take him long to pack his few pairs of clothes, his jacket and some other items as he kept a close eye out the window. Joe and Aunt Genevieve were coming out of the store looking distraught. Lucas threw his knapsack over his shoulder and escaped out of the house without anyone noticing.

"I can't believe it. I just can't!" Genevieve sank into a chair near the hearth in the kitchen. She could not escape the image of the empty register. Coralie fetched her a cup of water while Joe paced the floor and Isabelle stuffed her face with a piece of bread and jam, looking on as if nothing were wrong.

"I'm gonna report that good for nothing wretch to the police," Joe shouted, pushing open the back door and rushing out.

Genevieve took a long sip of water as she stared out the window. "How could Lucas do this to us?" she choked. "I don't understand how he could be so thoughtless and cruel."

Coralie pulled a chair next to her mother and placed a hand on hers. "How much did he steal, Mama?"

Genevieve's throat ached, and her eyes stung. "Everything in the register along with those expensive boots, two pocket knives and nearly all the candy."

"Oh," Coralie's voice was quiet. "How are we to make up for the loss?"

Genevieve had been wondering the same thing. They were already struggling to make ends meet. "I don't know, Coralie. Don't you fret about it. Everything will be fine," but she didn't quite believe herself.

A quarter of an hour later, Joe returned looking glum. His hair was disheveled from the run, and his face was twisted in a scowl as he angrily sank down into a chair. He mumbled something that was inaudible to

Genevieve. "Joe, please speak up. I can't understand you when you mumble so."

"The police are on the lookout for him," Joe said louder. "But he'll get away without a punishment and leavin' us in such a fix. I know it."

Genevieve swallowed and placed a hand on his shoulder. "Joe, we'll earn it back. I can take in some laundry or sewing work, and you'll work extra hard in the store, won't you?"

Joe didn't say anything and Genevieve turned her gaze to the fire.

How could you do this to us, Lucas?

Joe sat drowsily behind the counter in the store, leaning his chin on his fist. He hadn't slept at all the night before, and business had been unusually slow in the last hour. Any hope of leaving the store seemed lost to him now, for how could he leave the family with no one to look after the store?

Darn you, Lucas!

Joe was in such a foul mood that when Isabelle came in to spend the afternoon playing in the corner with her dolls, Joe grumbled at her. "Why can't you play somewhere else? You'll just sing and talk all afternoon and drive me insane."

"Mama said I could!" Isabelle whined. She settled herself in the corner and, to Joe's chagrin, started singing loudly and spun around with her doll, "All around the cobbler's house, the monkey chased the people, and after them in double haste. Pop goes the weasel!"

Joe buried his head in his arms and moaned.

"Joe, listen to this rhyme!" Isabelle ran over to him. Her face was aglow with excitement as she recited, "Hickory, dickory, dock, the mouse ran up the clock; the clock struck one, the mouse ran down; hickory, dickory, dock!" She stared at him with wide eyes, waiting to be praised for such an astonishing performance.

Joe patted her head. "You're a very clever little girl, Izzy," he said flatly.

She beamed and ran back to her corner to sing and rhyme some more.

Joe was relieved when the door opened, bringing in customers. It was Mrs. Elliott and her son, Levi.

"Good afternoon," Joe said, masking his ill humor.

"Good afternoon, Joseph," Mrs. Elliott said. She looked greatly concerned as she hurried over to the counter. "I was just in to visit your mother, and she told me what your cousin has done. I am so very sorry. I suppose deliveries will no longer be a service here?"

Joe shook his head. "Not unless I can convince Coralie to take my place behind the counter."

"Oh dear, no!" Mrs. Elliot's eyes grew wide from under her large bonnet. "It wouldn't be proper for a little

29

girl to work here all alone. But you can count on our business anyway, for the walk does us good."

"Thank you, Mrs. Elliott," Joe stifled a yawn.

Mrs. Elliot scanned the store. "I thought you were going to put up the war rally sign?"

"I don't think my mama would approve."

"Oh, I'm sure you're right, but it *is* such a noble cause."

"And along with doing something adventurous and patriotic, they also pay thirteen dollars a month," Levi said with a spark of excitement in his eyes.

Joe perked up as his friends spoke. It occurred to him that if he did join the army, he could send back his payments to restore the loss of what Lucas stole. "Are you enlistin', Levi?" Joe questioned, for an idea was brewing in his mind.

"No, indeed he is not!" Mrs. Elliott wrapped a protective arm around her boy. "He's just sixteen, and I already have two sons and a husband in the army. I think that's enough for now."

Joe grinned and looked from Mrs. Elliott to Levi. "Levi, how would you like to take a job here in the store?"

Chapter Four

The first gun is fired!
Its echoes thrill the land,
And the bounding hearts of the patriot throng,
Now firmly take their stand.
— George F. Root

Joe slapped on his cap, pulled open the door then peered to the right and left to make sure no one was about. It was nearly noon and he was expected to run deliveries, but he had other plans. He slipped out of the stuffy store and a fresh April wind grazed his face. He was going to join the army. It sent a pulse of excitement through his body.

It was a damp morning, and the sky was thick with clouds. As he strolled down the road, Joe pictured his name on an enlistment paper. It would look smart, he imagined.

Joseph Alexander Roberts.

Yes, he knew it would look smart. He readjusted the sack on his back and turned his face to the sun. He was starting to wonder if he should have told Mama that he was enlisting.

No, she wouldn't allow it, and then I'd be cooped up in the store all my life.

When Joe arrived in town, the square was a flurry of excitement. Men, women and children cheered their way through the streets, weaving their way through carriages and horses, waving American flags and cheering at the top of their lungs. The band played *The Star Spangled Banner* as politicians and town elders gathered on the gazebo in the middle of the park, shaking hands and exchanging polite words. Flowering crabapple trees sent off an enjoyable whiff of sweetness that helped overcome the scent of horse manure in the street.

Joe moved into the crowd beside a boy a few years his senior. He had never seen the little town so alive before. He leaned against a tree and felt the bark scratch his fingertips as he looked around in awe.

A tall man in a suit with a long narrow face and mustache made a gesture for the band to cease. He took off his hat and stepped forward to give a speech. His face was red with emotion, and his eyes bulged as he raised a fist and belted out his message, "Citizens of Westmoreland County, can we ignore the conflict that ensued at Fort Sumter in Charleston Harbor?"

Joe's heart started to swell in pride as the crowd lifted their fists and replied with a hearty, "No!"

"Citizens of Westmoreland County, will we stand by and allow the Union to fall into the hands of those Southern Rebels?"

This time, Joe joined in with the exuberant crowd and cried at the top of his lungs, "No!"

"Citizens of Westmoreland County, President Lincoln has asked for volunteers to stand up and defend the Union. Will the men of Westmoreland County run from the call of honor?"

"No!" Joe shouted, not holding back.

Joe's heart was racing, and his palms were sweating something fierce. He never knew that he had such a streak of patriotism in his blood!

"We, men of Westmoreland County, must rise, defend the Union and end the Southern Rebellion! Join the ranks! It will only take a mere three months to end it. This is your chance, men, to be a part of something that you can tell your children, grandchildren, and great-grandchildren. You can tell them, men of Westmoreland County, that you put the unlawful Southern boys in their place!"

As everyone was bellowing, the band started playing *The First Gun is Fired* while a man handed out music sheets. The music was penetrating and it stirred Joe's heart into its own rally. The crowd's patriotic spirits swelled in a chorus of,

The first gun is fired!

May God protect the right!

Let the freeborn sons of the North arise

In power's avenging night;

Shall the glorious Union our fathers have made,

By ruthless hands be sunder'd,

And we of freedom sacred rights

By trait'rous foes be plunder'd?

33

Arise! arise! arise!
And gird ye for the fight,
And let our watchword ever be,
"May God protect the right!"

The first gun is fired!
Its echoes thrill the land,
And the bounding hearts of the patriot throng,
Now firmly take their stand;
We will bow no more to the tyrant few,
Who scorn our long forbearing,
But with Columbia's stars and stripes
We'll quench their trait'rous daring.

The first gun is fired!
Oh, heed the signal well,
And the thunder tone as it rolls along
Shall sound oppression's knell;
For the arm of freedom is mighty still,
But strength shall fail us never,
Its strength shall fail us never,
That strength we'll give to our righteous cause,
And our glorious land forever.

Another man, shorter, with a round face and donning a pair of spectacles stood, "Men of Westmoreland County, a volunteer company of soldiers is being formed under Captain Richard Coulter. Step forward men and join! Let us fight for victory!"

The young man next to Joe sprang forward and took long, pride-filled strides to the enlistment roll that was set out in front of the gazebo on a wooden table. Everyone cheered as the young man signed his name. "That's it, my boy!" the man with the spectacles shouted. "Follow your brother's courage and honor, men, and enlist in the Union Army!"

Before Joe knew what was happening, his feet were taking him up to the enlistment roll. He was in a daze as everyone cheered him on. He bit the inside of his cheek until he tasted blood, then picked up the pen and signed his name. The next steps would prove challenging, he realized after reading the paper carefully. It wasn't a legal enlistment paper. He would need to sign up legally at the recruitment office, see a physician and be at least eighteen years old. He would have to convince Mama to sign for him or lie about his age.

No. I won't be a liar like Lucas. I have more honor than him.

When Joe walked into his house after the war rally, the scent of roast chicken greeted his nose. He could see Mama through the crack in the kitchen door. She was basked in light as she moved back and forth, preparing supper and humming softly to herself. She must have heard him walk in, for she was at the door in an instant, pushing a loose hair from her forehead. "Joe, I found this on the floor in the store." She held the war rally poster in her hand. "Is that where you were this morning?"

"Yes, ma'am," Joe's heart was beating hard inside his chest. He didn't want Mama to say no. She just *had* to let him go or he would go mad, he was sure of it.

"This war is for *men* to fight, Joe. Please leave it be." Mama looked worried as she set a thin hand on his shoulder.

Joe's fists clenched as rebellion swept over him without warning. "I'm gonna join the army. I won't stay here and be stuck in that store all my life, Mama. Can't you see? You seem to think I'm just a boy, but I'm not!" He was breathing hard.

Mama looked taken aback for a moment, and her eyes grew wistful. She clasped her hands together and pursed her lips tightly before speaking. "Joseph, you are only sixteen years—"

"Mama, it ain't fair!" he interrupted. "Lucas doesn't do a lick of work but he gets away with lyin' and stealin'. If it wasn't for him, Papa would still be here, and you can't deny that fact!"

"Joe, you must have some pity on Lucas—"

"Pity? Yes, I'm very sorry that Aunt Caroline and Uncle Simeon died, Mama, don't think I'm not. But why does Lucas get pitied after all the awful things he's done and continues to do? I've been a good son and brother and I ain't stole nothin' or been drinkin' or gotten into fist fights."

Mama stared at Joe and blinked, her eyes growing wet. "Joe—"

"You let him get away with anythin' because he's had a hard life. Well, so have I!" Joe brushed past his mother and shot upstairs, letting his footsteps sound twice as loud as usual.

"Joe! Open the door, would you?" Coralie could hardly keep her wobbly voice in check. She had been at the top of the staircase when she heard Joe and Mama's argument. Mama often said that Coralie was Joe's little shadow. Coralie knew it was true. She respected her brother greatly. She took his side in all matters, especially concerning Lucas, but now Joe was going batty and joining the army!

What's wrong with him? Has he lost all sense? She wondered as she pounded on the door.

"Go away!" Joe yelled.

She only pounded harder until her knuckles were sore and red. "Joe, please let me in!"

"I said go away!"

37

She didn't heed him. Coralie pushed open his door and stepped inside the small bedroom. Her eyes smarted, and her throat felt tight. "Oh, Joe how could you?"

He didn't answer. He was lying on his stomach and staring out the window.

"Why are you doing this? Why are you leaving us here alone? Mama, Izzy and I will have to run the store by ourselves now!"

"Coralie, I'm leavin' and that's that. I ain't gonna be a delivery boy at the store no more. I want to be a soldier and preserve the Union."

"You're cruel!" Coralie choked on her tears and tasted the saltiness of them on her tongue as they fell. "I don't care that Lucas left us but *you*, Joe? I never in my life imagined *you* abandoning us! What would Papa say?"

"I'm sorry. I truly am. But you just don't understand, Coralie. I have to get away."

I have a mind to slap Joe for being so selfish! Coralie glowered as she crossed her arms.

Joe stood up, grabbed his knapsack and set a firm hand on Coralie's shoulder. "Everythin' will be all right, Coralie. The war won't last long. I just *have* to be a part of it. If I don't join now, it'll be over, and I'll miss a great adventure."

Coralie pulled herself away from him and marched toward the window with her back to Joe. "I think you are being selfish and conceited, Joseph Roberts. Just look at you, seeking adventure and self glory over family and duty!" She turned to look at her brother.

"I'm sorry you feel that way, Coralie, but you ain't gonna change my mind."

The sun shining in from the window sent shafts of late afternoon light around the room, settling itself on Joe's desk as he strode out the door without so much as a glance back.

Joe found Isabelle sitting on the floor in the kitchen. She was pretending to read a book to her rag doll, and he had to grin when he saw her. Isabelle's hair was coming loose from its braids and her face was covered with chocolate as she scolded her doll for not listening to her. "Jenny, you *must* listen to this story, or I'll stuff you in the closet and you'll get no hot chocolate." She looked up when Joe walked in.

"Did Mama make you hot chocolate, Izzy?" he ruffled her hair and knew the answer to his question by the state of her dirty face.

Isabelle nodded with a grin as Joe leaned over and kissed her rosy cheek. "Bye, Izzy. Be a good girl and help Mama with chores, all right?"

She didn't seem to realize what was happening and simply smiled, giving him a slobbery kiss on the cheek. "Okay. Bye, Joe!"

Joe then found himself wandering to the parlor where he was sure to find Mama. He hesitated in the doorway for a moment. His heart tightened as he saw her sitting in front of the fireplace, looking so small and alone in that big chair that Papa used to sit in. Her brown hair looked almost red in the glow of the fire, and she worked busily, mending a rip in Isabelle's frock.

"Mama," he said softly.

She turned and quickly wiped a tear from her face. "Joe, come sit with me for awhile."

He set his knapsack near the carved walnut sofa before walking over to Mama and sitting in front of the fireplace. She smiled down at him as she set her mending aside.

"I'm sorry about earlier, Mama."

"I know you are. You're a good boy, Joe."

"Mama, I'm on my way to the recruitment office and I–I wanted to say a proper goodbye."

"Oh," Mama stared into the fire and tried to appear stoic, but Joe knew that he was breaking her heart. That in turn, broke his heart.

"Joe," Mama studied him, her face pale. "Do you even know anything about this war?"

He peered down and pulled a fraying string on his coat. "Sure I do. The South is tryin' to make their own country and withdraw from the Union. President Lincoln needs men to end the rebellion which won't take but three months. It's my duty to help preserve the Union at all costs. Just let me join, Mama, and I'll be back to work in the store for you. I promise. Let me do somethin' excitin' for once!"

"Oh, Joe," Mama ran a hand over his head of short, curly brown hair. "I'm so torn by this war. Of course I don't want to see the Union dissolve, but neither do I want to see my son march off with a gun. Please," Mama begged with tears in her eyes, "I don't think you should go."

Joe sighed heavily and felt that he would certainly have to lie to enlist. He was hoping that he could persuade Mama to sign the paper for him, but she wouldn't budge, it would appear. He stared into the snapping fire. Mama tapped her fingers nervously on the arm of her chair and didn't say anything for a long moment. The grandfather clock in the corner of the room tick-tocked and mingled with the crackling fire. The scent of burning wood was thick in Joe's nose as he tried to think of what to say next.

"All right, Joe. I'll sign for you, if you're sure this is what you need to do," Mama said suddenly.

Joe couldn't believe his ears. He sprang up, nearly knocking over the lamp on the end table behind him but caught it just in time. "Thank you, Mama! You'll be proud of me, I promise."

Mama nodded as Joe helped her to her feet. She clung to his sleeve and looked up at him with both sorrow and tenderness in her eyes. After a deep breath and a heartsick smile she said, "Well, let me fetch my shawl, and we'll go into town."

The dirt road was muddy from a fresh spring rain, and the air smelled damp. Joe dodged a puddle and assisted Mama around it. The hem of her skirt dusted the murky water, but she didn't say a word. Joseph's stomach twisted, and he thought he might vomit.

I, Joe Roberts, am about to join the army. The army!

His hands were buried in his pockets as he searched for the sign of the recruitment office. He didn't have to look far, for a crowd was gathered outside of it. American flags danced through the sky, and a band was playing a heart stirring tune. Joe got swept up in the music and began clapping.

Stand up for Uncle Sam, my boys,

With hearts brave and true.

Stand up for Uncle Sam, my boys,

For he has stood up by you.

He's made your homes the brightest
The sun o'er shone upon.
For honor, right and freedom,
He's many a battle won.

Oh, strike for Uncle Sam, my boys,
For danger is near.
Yes; strike strike for Uncle Sam, my boys,
And all to you most dear,

Oh, fall for Uncle Sam, my boys,
If need be to save.
Yes; fall for Uncle Sam, my boys,
Tho' in a soldier's grave.

His flag so long our glory
Dishonor'd shall not be
But heav'nward float forever
The banner of the free.

He heard Mama chuckle nervously and spun around to see her staring at him. "Joe, would you laugh if I told you something?"

Joe shrugged with mischief in his eyes. "I might, Mama."

She grinned and whispered, "With all of this excitement and patriotic music, I almost wish I could join!"

Joe burst into laughter at the thought of Mama wanting to join the army. Yet, he knew she was only trying to put on a brave face. He had seen tears flooding her eyes, but she wasn't one to cry in front of strangers, and so, she must do something to keep herself from it. He knew her well, so he went along with it. "Yes, you'd make an excellent officer, Mama!"

The recruitment office was a whirlwind of activity as men and boys jammed into the small space, their faces beaming with patriotic pride. It smelled strongly of sweat, which induced Mama to cover her nose with a handkerchief. The line moved fast and gave Joe little time to think about what he was doing and for Mama to let her emotions show. His hand was shaking as he put pen to paper and scrawled his name. Then he handed the pen to Mama, who held her head high as she grasped the pen firmly and signed her name - *Genevieve Florence Roberts* - in elegant, flowing handwriting.

"You will now report for a medical examination, then report to Camp Curtin in Harrisburg tomorrow," the captain behind the desk ordered.

The physician's office was only a few blocks away but the line that flooded into the street was going to take hours. "Since you don't have to report to Camp Curtin until tomorrow, why don't you come home for supper and stay the night? You can leave early in the morning, and I'll have time to pack you some food," Mama said.

Joe nodded with a smile of gratitude. "All right. I'll be home as soon as I can."

As Mama strolled down the road toward home, Joe wondered if she would shed a few tears once past the crowds, but he pushed that thought out of his mind as soon as it came. He hated when Mama cried.

The line outside the physician's office hadn't moved so Joe found a bench and sank down. He rested there for a moment and let the wind blow on his face as he closed his eyes and thought over what just happened.

This mornin' I was just a delivery boy, and now I'm off to be a soldier.

"Get outta my way!"

Joe's stomach churned as he sensed a familiar voice. He opened his eyes to find Lucas pushing his way through the crowded road, his boots shuffling on the dirt road. Lucas' pants were encrusted with mud, his cravat was lopsided, and his wool coat needed a good airing.

"Lucas!" Joe sprang to his feet and looked around wildly, as if by shouting his name the police would arrive.

Lucas' head jerked up, searching for who had called him. Their eyes locked, and Joe saw anger brewing in his cousin's glare. As Joe made a move toward Lucas, Lucas made a run for it. He slipped into the crowd and vanished from sight. Joe wouldn't give up. Not now, when he was so close. He picked up his pace, fueled by his anger, and finally spotted his cousin's curly head.

Joe reached out and snagged Lucas' arm, sending him falling to the ground in a cloud of dust. Lucas was upon his feet in an instant, hatred in his devilish eyes. He threw a fist toward Joe, who reeled from the blow and felt pain burn on the side of his face. Joe was quick to assault back, flying into Lucas' jaw with all his might. His hand stung from the force, and he inwardly groaned as his mind gleaned what was happening.

I'm becomin' like Lucas, fightin' like this!

Just as Lucas was stepping toward him with a fist raised, Joe was yanked away from the fight. The world spun around him and blurred into a mesh of colors and sounds, like a horrible dream.

"Boys! Save the fighting for the Rebels!" the man who had pulled Joe away shouted in his face. Joe shook himself free, snatched his bag and ran off, not quite sure where he was going as his face continued to sting.

He decided he would wait somewhere else until the line grew shorter.

Chapter Five

A score of millions hear the cry
And herald it abroad,
To arms they fly to do or die
For liberty and God.
— E. P. Dyer

Coralie watched out of the corner of her eye as Mama applied a wet cloth to Joe's face in the kitchen. Blood had dried on his mouth and cheeks, and he smelled of dirt and perspiration. She took a sip of water and kept an eye on her brother. "The doctor signed your enlistment paper, saying you were healthy, with blood all over your face?" Coralie asked incredulously.

Joe tried to turn and look at her, but Mama pushed his head back. "Stay still, Joe," she scolded.

Joe sat up straight with a grin. "I told him he should see what I did to Lucas' face. The doctor laughed and said I was a fine, strong young man."

Mama shook her head as she dipped the cloth into a basin of water and wrung it out. "Joe, how could you get into a fight with your cousin? Yes, he did wrong by stealing, but you needn't stoop to his level and start acting like him. You said just this morning that you didn't get into fights, and now look at you!"

Joe gazed sheepishly at the ground while Coralie pouted. He would be leaving at dawn, and she told herself that she didn't care.

Let him go and be a fool. I can't stop him.

She picked up a book that was lying on a stool and hid her face in it. The paper smelled old and cracked under her fingertips. She didn't know what the book was about, but it was a good hideaway.

"What's wrong with Lucas anyhow? He's nothin' but a nuisance, and he's been like that since he came to live with us," Joe winced as Mama set the cloth on his cheek.

Coralie's mind wandered as she pretended to read the book. She remembered the day when Lucas came. She was nine years old. He looked so cold and unfriendly with his dark eyes and scowling face. She was rather frightened of him. Many nights she would hear the front door open, bringing Lucas home in a drunken stupor and blackeyed from a brawl. Her parents would always be waiting for him, and she would hear Papa and Lucas arguing late into the night.

"Just have patience with Lucas. He's–he's troubled," Mama's voice sounded strained, but she regained her composure again as she patted Joe on the shoulder. "There, you're all cleaned up and presentable again except for that bruise under your eye, but that will heal soon enough." She picked up the basin of water and poured it out the open window. "Go wash your hands for supper, you two, while I get Izzy cleaned up."

When Mama left the room to find Isabelle, silence wrapped around the kitchen, causing every small noise to sound like thunder. The floorboards creaked, and the wind whistled through the window making the curtains softly dance. The fire snapped, mingling with the faint sound of Isabelle's footsteps from upstairs. Joe shifted in his seat. Coralie looked up and caught him staring at her and swiftly peered down at her book again.

"Stop that, Coralie."

She calmly lifted her eyes and shut the book. The fragrance of old paper drifted around her face as she did so. "Stop what?"

"Glarin' at me," Joe's fingers brushed the bruise under his eye. "Do I look beaten up pretty badly?"

He didn't look horrible, but Coralie found herself nodding. "You aren't as strong as you think, Joe. You'd better stay home until you are stronger, don't you think?"

"Coralie, you're not gonna change my mind." He leaned forward in his chair, and his brown eyes bore into her. "Do you understand?"

It sounded as if he were explaining something to four year old Isabelle and not a thirteen year old. Coralie stood up as her chair screeched against the floor. "No, Joe. I don't understand. Tell Mama that I won't be joining the family for supper tonight. I'm not feeling well."

A soft knock sounded on Coralie's door in the morning. She was already awake, dressed, and sitting by the window, waiting to watch Joe leave. She hadn't spotted him yet. Coralie had an inkling that it was Joe knocking on the door, but she didn't want to talk to him. Her eyes remained fixed on the maple tree right outside her window. The leaves were the fresh, tender green of spring, and they waved gently in the wind. Her eyes wandered to their store which lay beyond the tree. She could just make out the sign through the leaves. Joe hadn't fixed the faded lettering.

"Coralie, if you don't open the door, I'll knock it down," came Joe's low voice.

Coralie knew he would keep his word, so she unlocked the door and slowly pulled it open. Joe stood there all dressed and ready for the day, his hair combed and almost smooth, if not for his stubborn curls.

"Yes?" Coralie asked.

"I'm leavin', and I wanted to say goodbye."

Coralie sucked in a breath and tried to remain indifferent. "Yes, well, goodbye." She turned as her eyes and nose stung from oncoming tears.

I will not cry. Don't you dare cry, Coralie Roberts.

"For goodness sake, I'll be back in three months! The war might be over even before that, who knows, so just stop your mopin'," Joe chided her.

Three months was a long time without Joe. Coralie crossed her arms and faced the window. Abruptly she felt two hands whirl her around, and she was suddenly in front of Joe. He planted his hands firmly on her

50

shoulders, so she couldn't turn her back toward him again. "Now you just listen to me, you young whippersnapper. I have to leave, or I'll go mad. You know how I get when I go mad, don't you?" He smirked, which made Coralie grin in spite of herself. "I've asked Mrs. Elliott if Levi would come work at the store while I'm gone, so you'll have help. I'll be back soon, and then I'll take over again for a while before my next adventure. How does that sound?"

Coralie shrugged. Levi Elliott was an improvement over Lucas, but he could never take the place of Joe. "You better come home right quick, Joe Roberts."

He smiled. "I will, Coralie. You take care of yourself and Mama and Izzy. You be strong, all right?"

She nodded and tried with all her might to keep the tears safely in her eyes. The wetness clouded her vision, and she saw only a blurry figure leave and close the door.

It was evening and a light sheet of rain fell. The dampness wasn't pleasant to Joe's weary bones as he stepped off the train into Harrisburg. He was tired, and the noise flooded his ears – the loud voices of the men, the whistle's cry, and the constant rumble of the train cars. He longed for some peace and quiet. Stuffing his hands into his pockets, he joined a group of men in the newly formed company from town. He shuffled silently through Harrisburg as the wet streets shimmered in the moonlight.

When they arrived at Camp Curtin, Joe was surprised that it was just a large, old fairground. Hundreds of white Sibley tents were in neat rows, and Joe could see smoke from campfires billowing into the night air. It smelled welcoming and he began to feel more at ease.

Joe and his company were taken by a sergeant to a building near the back of camp to be mustered into service. He sincerely wished they were in uniform, for it would make the mustering in look much more impressive. He swallowed hard as he realized there was no going back. He lifted his hand and said, "I, Joseph Alexander Roberts, do solemnly swear that I will bear true allegiance to the United States of America, and that I will serve them honestly and faithfully against all their enemies and opposers whatsoever, and observe and obey the orders of the President of the United States, and the orders of the officers appointed over me according to the rules and articles of the government of the armies of the United States."

Joe felt a strange sensation run through his veins. Excitement and...fear.

Now I'm a real soldier.

One more emotion was added to the mix when Joe happened to look down the line of soldiers and saw Lucas standing there. Joe gaped, then shook his head in disbelief.

It would have been bad enough for Lucas to be in the same regiment as me, but the same company is too much!

Joe pushed his way through the company to confront his cousin. Lucas looked just as surprised as Joe felt. His eyes widened when he saw Joe. Then he muttered under his breath, "You gotta be kiddin' me."

"Ain't this a *pleasant* surprise, meetin' up here?" Joe flung his hands up in disgust.

"What are you doin' here?" growled Lucas.

"I should be askin' *you* the same question," Joe spat. "You should be in prison after what you did to my family. If I thought the army would do somethin' about lockin' you up, I'd turn you in this very minute."

Lucas raised an eyebrow, "I think the army has more important matters on its mind right now. If I had known you were gonna do a fool thing like enlist, I would have enlisted in another regiment."

"Just stay away from me, Lucas," Joe sneered as they tramped through the chilly night across the field.

"Gladly."

Joe stormed away from his cousin as they neared their regiment's tents. Men were sitting around campfires, their soft voices and laughter carried on the wind.

"Twelve men to each tent," the sergeant barked, handing them each a thin, flimsy blanket. "You'll get your food rations tomorrow," then he left them.

Joe peeked into his tent, not quite believing twelve men could fit inside. As he looked, he noticed that there was a cone shaped stove right in the middle to keep them warm. He was sore from the train ride and tired from a restless night's sleep. He stumbled into the tent and wrapped himself in the scratchy blanket. He lay there, feet close to the meager stove as he tried to ward off the damp air. Eleven men filed in behind him, their faces unfamiliar. It didn't take long for the jesting to cease and be replaced by snores. Joe jammed his fingers into his ears and burrowed beneath the thin blanket. One of the men was mumbling in his sleep, so Joe lay on his stomach and tried to tune it out.

A breeze crept under the tent and bit Joe's face with its sharp coldness. The ground was dank and seeped into his blanket, causing his feet to be numb and the tip of his nose to feel like ice. He finally rolled over once more and stared up at where the stove pipe slipped through a small opening for ventilation. Joe wondered how Coralie, Isabelle and Mama were faring. If he was home, he would be in his soft bed, wrapped in the three quilts that Mama had made and in his quiet room by himself.

Stop it, Joe, he suddenly rebuked himself. *You wanted to join the army, and now you're here.*

A loud snore startled him, and he glared into the darkness. He ardently wished he could stuff a blanket into the snorer's big mouth.

Chapter Six

"Every officer and soldier, who is able to do duty, ought to be busily engaged in military preparation by hard drilling in order that through the blessing of God, we may be victorious in the battles, which in his all-wise providence may await us."
– Stonewall Jackson

Joe burrowed into his blanket. The fabric felt rough on his face and smelled of mildew. He was drowsy, but he forced himself to open his eyes and found the tent to be wrapped in dark, inky shadows. He sat up. No one was awake yet, and immediately his hand flew to his nose. With so many bodies in close proximity to one another, the tent smelled putrid. Everything was moist, including Joe and his blanket. He thought he might be sick.

His heart gave a leap of exhilaration as music filled the still air. A bugle, sounding the tune of Reveille, induced the men to awaken, rub their eyes and yawn but mostly complain about their lack of sleep. Joe laughed wryly. *They* were the ones snoring the night away, while he tossed and turned.

He lifted the canvas flap of the tent, strolled out into the bleak morning air and studied his surroundings. The camp was swallowed in misty grey hues. All around him, men from the other companies of his regiment were stumbling out of their tents. From where Joe was standing he could see down to the city of Harrisburg that was wrapped in thick fog. The inhabitants were just awakening and opening their shops. He could see the flickering of candles shining through the windows, creating a homey feel in the midst of the darkness and cold. His eyes darted to the slate grey sky as crows hurried across overhead, cawing loudly and confidently as if *they* were assigned the task of waking the men with Reveille. In camp all he could see were tall white tents and men in flannel shirts, hair sticking up all over their heads. This wasn't what he imagined a training camp would be like.

I want a uniform, he kept thinking. *I want to fight.*

"Attention, men! Attention!" shouted a captain, who was pushing and pulling men into a line. "Company I of the 11th Pennsylvania Infantry Volunteers, attention!"

Joe stood still, looking up and down the line to see how the others were standing. Some had their shoulders back, feet spread apart, hands at their sides, while others slouched and stared down at the ground. The men didn't know what to do and were in need of breakfast by the looks of them.

Joe lifted his head and pulled his shoulders back. The men grew quiet as the captain paraded up and down the line, hands behind his back. The man wasn't very tall, but he held himself with an air of calm superiority. "I'm Captain Richard Coulter," he bellowed. "Welcome to the army, boys."

The drone of the other companies drilling around them nearly drowned out the bearded captain's words. He had to shout so loudly that his round face turned bright red. "You will stand with your feet turned out, knees

56

extended and shoulders back. Suck in your gut and puff out your chest. Arms at your side, head straight, eyes forward."

Joe tried to remember everything the captain was ordering, but when his memory failed him, he glimpsed the men beside him and imitated their movements. He felt strange standing there in such an unfamiliar position.

"When I say 'company, right, face,' you all will turn to the right," Captain Coulter continued. He stopped in front of a clumsy boy who looked not much older than Joe. "Suck in your gut, Private..."

"Oliver Willyard, sir," the boy answered and obeyed, his face turning red as a tomato.

"Breathe, Private Willyard!" Captain Coulter shouted at him. Oliver let out a breath with such a racket of wheezing that Joe couldn't help but snicker. Captain Coulter turned to glare at him, and Joe immediately grew silent.

"Company, left, face!"

They turned to the left, all except those who didn't know their right from their left, or had suddenly forgotten. Oliver Willyard was one of them.

They drilled for over an hour, and Joe's stomach began to growl. He could have shouted for joy when Captain Coulter announced that they were dismissed for breakfast and to retrieve their rations at Floral Hall which was at the far end of the camp. Joe was indignant when he discovered that his rations were raw beef and bread to be cooked on the tent's stove or on the campfires.

This ain't no breakfast, he grumbled to himself.

At home he would be having whatever he pleased, be it ham, bacon, biscuits, jam, butter, molasses...anything.

But Joe was hungry, and he had to admit that nothing tasted so good as that beef and bread as he sat around the smoky campfire. Someone had heated a kettle of water, and Joe added it to the coffee he had sprinkled into his mug. He took a long sip of the hot liquid and shuttered. It was his first time drinking coffee black. He didn't quite care for it but for some reason, he continued to drink it and shiver.

The meal ended at nine o'clock, and the company was formed into a line again as Captain Coulter stood before them. The sky behind his broad figure was clear blue, and not a cloud was to be seen. It was a good day for drilling, for even though Joe was fascinated with becoming a soldier, he knew it would be miserable to drill in the cold or pouring rain.

Captain Coulter cleared his throat before delivering the orders of Camp Curtin. The paper he held fanned in the wind, as he declared, "The following orders will be observed by the troops while in camp at Camp Curtin:

1. The Reveille will be sounded at the dawn of the day, and companies will form on the parade grounds, and as soon as the Reveille ceases, the rolls will be called by the Orderly Sergeants, superintended by a commissioned

officer, and immediately after roll call the companies will drill for one hour.

2. Immediately after company drill, the tents will be put in order by men of the companies, superintended by chiefs of squads; the parades, streets of the camp, etc, will be cleaned by the police party of the day, in charge of a non-commissioned officer, superintended by the officer of the guard.

3. Breakfast call will be sounded at seven o'clock.

4. The Troop will sound at half-past nine, a.m., for the purpose of guard mounting.

5. The first Sergeants will make their reports at Headquarters every morning, at ten o'clock.

6. Captains will be required to drill their companies from half-past ten to half-past eleven a.m., and from four to five, p.m.

7. The dinner call will be sounded at twelve o'clock.

8. The Retreat will be sounded at sunset, when the rolls will be called and orders of the day read.

9. The Tattoo will be sounded at nine o'clock in the evening, when the rolls will be called, and no soldier will be allowed to be out of his tent after this hour without special permission, and all lights will be extinguished at the tap of the drum.

10. Any soldier coming into camp intoxicated or bringing liquor in, will be immediately placed under arrest by the officer of the guard.

11. Any person selling liquor within the bounds of prescribed by law will be dealt with according to law in such cases made and prescribed.

Captains of companies will be held responsible for a strict observance of the above orders. By order of E. C. Williams, Brigadier General Commanding and Joseph F. Knipe, Aid de Camp."

And so went Joe's first day in the army.

Chapter Seven

"Let me tell you what is coming. After the sacrifice of countless millions of treasure and hundreds of thousands of lives you may win Southern independence, but I doubt it. The North is determined to preserve this Union. They are not a fiery, impulsive people as you are, for they live in colder climates. But when they begin to move in a given direction, they move with the steady momentum and perseverance of a mighty avalanche."
– Sam Houston

Joe sat by the smokey campfire with a group of men from his company. Some of the men were singing, while others talked and laughed so loudly that a private came out of his tent, groggy eyed and shouted at them for keeping him awake. Joe took a long sip of coffee, and it warmed him as it slipped down his throat.

Sitting next to him was the boy named Oliver Willyard, who was dubbed the clumsy "Jonah" of the company and two brothers, Will and Johnny Story, ages eighteen and nineteen.

"So, Roberts, why did you join the army?" Will Story asked.

Joe wrapped his hands around the tin mug of coffee and took another swig. "Not much to tell. I'm sixteen, and I needed to join the army to prove that I'm not some little boy anymore. I needed an adventure."

"Lordy," Will shook his head. "You're only sixteen? You *are* just a boy, Roberts."

Joe's eyes flew up, and he scowled at his new friend. "No, I ain't. I can fight just as good as you."

Will held up his hands in defense, "I didn't mean anything by it, Roberts. I only said that because Johnny and I have a younger brother who's sixteen. I just can't think of him joining up, is all."

"How many brothers and sisters do you have?" Joe asked, thinking of his own family.

"There's fourteen of us in all," Will said. "Six of us boys are in the army. Mother said that if we're going to join up we should do so in pairs, so we could take care of each other. So I'm here to take care of my older brother, Johnny."

"And I'm here to make sure my little brother here doesn't get shot by a Reb," Johnny said. "He's awfully *loud* if you haven't noticed. The Rebs will hear him a mile away!"

The conversation then turned to Oliver Willyard. Oliver took off his cap as he stared into the fire. "Me?" He twisted it in his hands. "Well, my pa and ma owned a store, and I worked at it with my brothers and sisters. But every time I went to get a customer a barrel of flour or coffee beans, I would spill it all over the place. It started to get sorta expensive – all the merchandise I wasted – and Pa said I should try being an apprentice for the newspaper instead. I spilled so much ink there that they sent me home, and I started to work at a farm outside of town. Wouldn't you know it? I nearly killed their dog, tripping over him while holding a pitchfork. So, I came home and decided to join the army. I think Pa and Ma were a bit worried about me, seeing as I'm a little clumsy."

As he said this, Oliver went to pour himself a cup of coffee and knocked the kettle into the fire. The liquid distinguished some of the flames with a loud sizzle.

"Oh, uh...oops," he looked around bashfully.

They could have been cross with him, but it was too ironic, and they all laughed which made Oliver grin slightly as he put the kettle back where it belonged.

Joe heard footsteps behind him and turned to find Lucas sauntering over, hands in his pockets. "Did you hear about my little cousin, Joe, yet? Sad little thing, ain't he? Just a boy. If he weren't here right now – by some miracle I might add – he would be home listenin' to his little sister play the piano while he sat near the warm fire. Or maybe playin' dolls with his baby sister, ain't that right, Joe?"

Joe clenched his jaw. He wanted to slug him. Punch him. Thrash him *hard*. Instead he gritted his teeth and took another sip of coffee.

Stay calm, Joe, stay calm.

63

Lucas settled himself on the ground near the fire and, for the moment, was the only one talking. "Joe used to follow me around like a little lost pup. He wanted to be *just* like me. And look! He even followed me to the army!" Lucas turned a lazy grin toward Joe, a dark look in his eyes. "I'm flattered!"

Joe sprang up, his fists clenched, but the Story brothers must have sensed his intentions because they each grabbed one of his arms and pulled him back. "Let it go, Roberts." It was a good thing he did, too, for the sergeant joined the group a moment later.

"And how is Company I doing?" the sergeant asked.

Joe kept his head down, for he knew if he saw that wicked grin on Lucas' face he might pound him.

"When are we gonna whip some Rebs is what I'd like to know," he heard Lucas say.

"All in good time, private."

Lucas had a habit of making friends with the thieves and troublemakers. He had escaped from one group merely to fall into another who immediately accepted him. It was Norm Adams and Pleasant Cunningham who had pulled him into their schemes. Norm and Pleasant revelled in making the lives of others miserable and apparently thought Lucas was the type to do the same.

The three of them had already scared the wits out of a man coming from his tent one morning by jumping out from behind another tent and howling at him. They'd beaten up one fellow who refused to give them his rations, and they gleefully poured mud into a coffee mug and gave it to a soldier, pretending it was freshly brewed coffee.

Lucas sat quietly as Norm and Pleasant scoffed at everyone and plotted new tricks to play on them. He wasn't paying close attention as he stared into the crackling evening fire. No one dared come talk to him and he was fine with that. Just fine. His mind drifted as his father's tanned face and dark eyes appeared in his head, complete with his usual apparel – a fine suit, a gold pocket watch and his tall, black hat.

"You are a disgrace to me, Lucas. A disgrace. Did you hear me, boy?" Lucas could still recall the feeling of his father's hand as it stung the side of his face. *"What do you mean by drinking and stealing and starting fights like a common criminal? I'm utterly ashamed of you!"* Another forceful blow across his face, his ears, his head. *"I'm grateful for this business trip to London, and you should be, too. If stayed here, I'd have a few more choice words for you, boy!"*

"Well, if you wouldn't abandon me all the time, I might respect you," Lucas had exploded, *"You're a miserable excuse for a father! You lock yourself away from me...sometimes I even wonder if I have a father."*

That earned him a grab by the ear, and he was dragged up into his bedroom and locked in. His father left the next day, and Lucas never saw him again. The ship bound for London had sunk, leaving Lucas alone with a mansion that he couldn't afford. His father had left him nothing in his will.

That's when he was sent to live with his Aunt Genevieve, Uncle Charles and his cousins.

"What's eating you, Holmes?" Pleasant asked, bringing Lucas out of his troublesome thoughts. "Did you see that Oliver Willyard fellow? What a dunce!" He obviously wasn't very interested in what was eating Lucas, for he kept on talking. "He was walking around camp today with his boots on the wrong feet!"

"Hey, I know what we could do," Norm drawled, glancing at the fire where Oliver, Joe and a few others sat a few feet away. "Let's fill his boots with mud when he takes them off this evening. Won't that be a nice surprise for him in the morning?"

"Let's do it," Lucas said, just to get his mind off his thoughts.

"What the devil?"

Joe turned as he was buttoning his coat and found Oliver on the other side of the tent. He was hopping on one foot and looking greatly confused.

"What's wrong with you, Willyard?" Joe asked. Oliver shot him a dark look, then followed it by giving all the men in the tent a glare. "All right, which one of you did this? It ain't funny. I've only got two pairs of socks, and the other pair is damp."

Joe walked over to Oliver and peered into his boot. It was filled with a glob of mud, and Oliver's socked foot was covered with it from heel to toe. All of the men were snickering, but each vowed that they didn't do it, which baffled Oliver. "One of you is lying!"

Joe chewed on the side of his cheek as he tried to think of who would do something like this. Most of the men in their company were nice fellows and respected each other's property and wouldn't go doing a fool thing like this. Well, except for Lucas and those two other characters he sat around with. "I'll betcha it was Lucas, Pleasant and Norm. They're always up to somethin'."

Oliver groaned as he pushed open the tent flap. "I'll whip the daylights outta them!"

Joe grabbed Oliver's shoulder and hauled him back. "Willyard, they'll eat you alive. You can't even put your shoes on the right feet."

Joe was fetching coffee that evening when he tripped over something and fell flat on his face. His tin mug bounced off the ground and rolled away from him. With a spit, he sat up and looked to see who or what had tripped him. Lucas smiled down at him and held out a hand. "Let me help you up, little cousin."

Joe threw him a glare and stood up, dusting the dirt from his shirt and pants. "Get outta here," he mumbled. "And quit pickin' on your fellow comrades. If you'd like to do that, join the confederacy."

"Oh, look at the tough Joe Roberts. I'm *so* touched by your speeches."

That did it. Joe couldn't hold himself back any longer. He lunged at Lucas, grabbing both of his shoulders and shoved him hard into the ground. Joe was on top of him for a moment, but Lucas suddenly gave him a hard thrust backward, and Joe's head slammed into a rock. His head rattled, and his vision blurred. The pain throbbed in Joe's skull, and his hands instinctively flew to his head. Lucas didn't seem to care, though blood began to stream from Joe's temple. He leapt on him and started pounding Joe, pinning him down so that he couldn't escape.

"Let me go!" Joe hollered weakly. He couldn't fight back. The torment to his head was dazing him. "Let me go, Lucas!" But Lucas wouldn't heed him. Joe tasted the rustiness of blood on his lips and sensed a sharp pain coming from his left arm. He was certain his cousin would seriously injure him. Maybe even kill him.

"Leave 'im alone, Holmes!" It was Oliver's voice and Joe groaned inwardly. Oliver was a good friend and all, but he was so small and skinny. He couldn't stand up against Lucas. Suddenly Joe felt himself being freed and could vaguely make out the image of Lucas being dragged off by First Lieutenant Terry.

Joe was laying on his back, looking up at the granite shaded sky while gasping for breath.

"Roberts, are you all right?"

Joe blinked. He couldn't make out the face. "What?"

"It's Sergeant Jones. Do you need a doctor?"

"No," Joe gasped, gripping his arm. "I'm all right." He looked down. His hand was dripping with blood.

"Your head looks pretty bad. How many fingers am I holding up?"

"Four? Three? I don't know." Everything was blurred into one form, and Joe closed his eyes, letting sleep take him away from the pain.

69

Chapter Eight

"Common sense is seeing things as they are;
and doing things as they ought to be."
— Harriet Beecher Stowe

Genevieve sank onto the edge of her bed. She took a few deep breaths as she unlaced her boots and rubbed her sore feet. Levi Elliott was a good worker to have around the store, but without Joe, who knew the ins and outs of it so well, Genevieve was left with much of the work along with her household duties and taking care of two daughters.

You couldn't keep him here, she told herself. *Joe will learn and come back a different boy.* She only prayed he was changed for the good.

She pulled out the pins from her hair and made a pile of them on her dressing table as her thick brown hair fell in a heap around her shoulders and down to her waist. Her eyes fell on the daguerreotype of herself and her late husband, Charles. It was taken after Joe was born, and she was holding the curly haired boy in her arms. She wished they had gotten their likeness taken after Isabelle was born so that the entire family would be captured together, but there hadn't been enough time.

Tears burned in her eyes and caused her throat to swell.

She looked once more at the photograph and stared at her husband, noticing that Joe was starting to resemble him as he grew up. They both had handsome brown eyes and that mischievous grin. It was too much on her heart, looking at that photograph. She snatched the daguerreotype and headed for the trunk at the foot of her bed. Kneeling on the hardwood floor, she pulled the trunk open and delicately set it in an old hat box as a tear ran down her cheek.

Lord, please give me strength to endure this.

As she was closing the hat box, her eyes fell on an envelope with her name written in flowing cursive. Nostalgia swept over Genevieve as she unfolded a letter from the year 1844. It was from Lucas' mother – her sister, Caroline. She had completely forgotten about it.

Dear Sister….

Joe and his company stood and waited for drill orders in their homespun shirts looking like a group of awkward men whose footing, gun holdings and posture would make a veteran soldier cringe.

"Where was Lucas taken?" Joe whispered to Oliver.

"He was bucked and gagged. I also heard he had to sit extra long like that 'cause he mouthed back to

Lieutenant Terry. I wouldn't want to run into him today. He's probably in an awful mood."

Joe could still feel the pain in his arm and head from his run in with Lucas. He most certainly did not wish to see Lucas today or ever again.

"Order arms!" Captain Coulter shouted.

They were supposed to hold the Springfield rifle parallel against them, but it was challenging for Joe. His arm burned everytime he moved it.

"Shoulder arms!"

Joe grabbed the rifle with his right hand and held it up against himself. The gun was so heavy that his arms felt like clay by the time Captain Coulter called, "Present arms!"

He brought the rifle in front of him and held it there, gritting his teeth and glancing to the right of him. Oliver Willyard dropped his rifle and was scampering to pick it up when Captain Coulter stood in front of him.

"Private Willyard!"

"Y-yessir?" Oliver sputtered.

"I said *present arms!*"

Oliver quickly held his gun in front of him and looked straight ahead. When Captain Coulter turned his back, Joe let his rifle rest on the ground. His arms fell to his side like rubber.

"Private Roberts!"

Joe picked up his rifle. His heart was thudding inside him. "Sir?"

"If I find you resting your rifle again, you'll be drilling while your comrades are eating. Am I understood, private?"

Joe nodded. "Yes, sir."

May 1861

"Lordy, it's cold as the arctic!" Joe said the next morning as Reveille sounded. His socks were damp and icy, and he was shivering. The ground was covered with six inches of slushy snow, and a cold breeze whipped at his face as he stepped out of the tent. He felt like huddling into a ball and hibernating until May started acting like May and not December. But there was no time to dawdle. They had received orders the night before that they were moving out of Camp Curtin and headed for another camp in West Chester. Joe's belongings didn't take long to pack, and since they still hadn't been given uniforms, he wore his old flannel shirt that smelled so ghastly that it made his nose twitch.

They marched out of Camp Curtin and down the streets of Harrisburg, back to the railroad from whence they came. This time there were people cheering them on. Joe glanced around at the civilians who came out of their homes in spite of the cold. He spotted a girl who resembled Coralie, and Joe's heart skipped a beat.

74

Don't look back, don't look back.

But he did. She smiled at him, but it wasn't Coralie. It was some other girl whose brother or father had left to serve his country.

"Go get those Rebs!" one woman shouted.

"God save the Union!" a man said.

Joe couldn't help but smile amidst the brisk air that wrapped around him.

"Too bad we're not in uniform," Oliver said to Joe as they marched. "We'd look a good deal better."

Joe had to agree. They didn't look too fierce at the moment.

A middle aged woman came running out of her house with blankets in her arms and started calling out to them, "Boys! Take these and keep warm! God be with you."

Joe gratefully took a blanket and nodded his thanks. It was made of thick wool. He wished he had it last evening when the air was so cold that he couldn't feel his fingers or toes. They marched on toward the station as the sound of the whistle echoed off store fronts. Joe found a double seat aboard the train with Oliver Willyard and the Story brothers.

"Heard we're going to a camp called Wayne," Johnny said.

"When are we gonna do some fightin'?" Joe asked, turning to look out the window. The train was still boarding, and the station was clogged with soldiers.

"I don't mind going to another camp," Oliver said, taking off his cap. His head of thick brown hair fell limp in the cold. "I'm none too eager to meet up with the Rebs."

"Then why on earth did you the join the army?" Will asked.

Oliver sighed and threw his hands up in exasperation. "I *told* you why already, Will Story!"

The train slowly puffed out of the station. Joe saw Harrisburg disappear into a cloud of smoke and fog. "What do you think enemy country is like?" Joe asked.

Oliver shrugged and looked across at Will and Johnny. "I don't know. You two ever been down south?"

"Nah," Johnny said. "But I hear it's darn right hot and sticky. They have rattlesnakes, too. I don't know why anyone would go down there, truth be told. But we'll be seeing it before too long."

"I bet they don't have snow in May," Joe snickered. The window of the train was icy. He wiped it with the back of his sleeve to see the fields of wet snow whirl past them.

Will leaned in and motioned toward Lucas who was sitting across the aisle from them. "So, you're related to him?"

"Unfortunately." Joe glanced over at his cousin. "Our mothers were sisters, but thankfully we don't look a thing alike."

Oliver looked from Lucas to Joe then shrugged. "I don't know about that. You both have curly hair."

Joe refused to have anything in common with Lucas, and so he ran his hand over his head saying indignantly, "My hair is *not* curly." But he knew it was. He had it cut short but no matter what he did to it, no matter what foolish, newfangled hair tonic he tried, it still was curly. As was Lucas', much to Joe's chagrin.

"Why don't you two get along?" Johnny asked, crossing his arms behind his head.

Joe sighed, leaning back in his seat. "He came to live with us four years ago and had a habit of breakin' the law and doing whatever he wanted. One night he didn't come home, and so my father went after him." Joe looked down at his shoes. "Lucas was in a bad fight, and my father tried to break it up, but he...he got thrown to the cobblestone ground so hard that he died. I ain't been able to forgive him for that, nor anythin' else he's done to make our lives miserable."

The boys didn't say anything for a moment until Will leaned back in his seat. "Maybe you'll learn to deal with each other in the army."

Joe shook his head. "No way. There's no reasoning with him. Never."

Chapter Nine

The Union forever! Hurrah, boys, hurrah!
Down with the traitors, up with the stars;
While we rally round the flag, boys, rally once again,
Shouting the battle cry of freedom!
— George F. Root

Camp Wayne, West Chester, Pennsylvania

It was bleak outdoors, but there was no snow. Joe hunched his shoulders against the chill and willed his arms to pour a mug of coffee. Once he had a sip of the warm beverage, he retrieved a sheet of paper and pen and started to write, using his knee as a table.

Dear Mama, Coralie and Izzy,

I apologize for not writing in a long while. Drilling is all we do at the moment...well, I shouldn't say that. At Camp Wayne we do have some free time in the early evenings, and at this moment (it's almost six), the men are playing leapfrog and corner ball. I'm itching for a battle. I've made some friends, I suppose, but Lucas being in the same regiment as me has provided some challenges. I wish I had some great story to tell about the army, but nothing's happened. We're stationed at Camp Wayne for a spell, so write to me if you have time. Direct your letters to:

Private Joseph A. Roberts,
Company I, 11th Pennsylvania Infantry Volunteers,
Camp Wayne, West Chester, Pennsylvania.

Yours always,

Joe

At eight-thirty that evening, the men all gathered around camp fires again. Joe emerged from the tent and stopped to look around. The camp really was pleasant looking with all the fires sending sparks into the starry sky. The musician of the company, Augustus Smith, played a mockery version of the southern song, "Dixieland," and Joe found himself grinning as he listened.

Away down South in the land of traitors,

Rattlesnakes and alligators,

Right away, come away, right away, come away.

Where cotton's king and men are chattels,

Union boys will win the battles,

Right away, come away, right away, come away.

Then we'll all go down to Dixie,

Away, away,

Each Dixie boy must understand

That he must mind his Uncle Sam,

Away, away,

And we'll all go down to Dixie.

Away, away,

And we'll all go down to Dixie.

I wish I was in Baltimore,

I'd make Secession traitor's roar,

Right away, come away, right away, come away.

We'll put the traitors all to rout.

I'll bet my boots we'll whip them out,

Right away, come away, right away, come away.

Then we'll all go down to Dixie,

Away, away,

Each Dixie boy must understand

That he must mind his Uncle Sam,

Away, away,

And we'll all go down to Dixie.

Away, away,

And we'll all go down to Dixie.

Oh, may our Stars and Stripes still wave

Forever o'er the free and brave,

Right away, come away, right away, come away.

And let our motto ever be –

For Union and for Liberty!

Right away, come away, right away, come away.

Then we'll all go down to Dixie,

Away, away,

Each Dixie boy must understand

That he must mind his Uncle Sam,

Away, away,

And we'll all go down to Dixie.

Away, away,

And we'll all go down to Dixie.

"Coralie, why don't you pen a letter to Joe and Lucas today? I'm sure they would appreciate hearing from you."

"I'd rather not, Mama. I don't have anything to say." Coralie sat in the parlor with her nose in a book as Mama and Isabelle were writing letters. She glanced over Isabelle's shoulder and saw two stick figures being formed on paper with big letters that read *Joe and Izzy eeting caak.*

"For heaven's sake, Izzy, do you think Joe will know what you mean by 'eeting caak'?" she scolded her sister.

"Yes, he will!" Isabelle gave her a defiant look as she kept on working. She gripped the pencil with her chubby fingers and started humming.

"Coralie, leave your sister alone. If you're not going to pen a letter, then continue reading your book." Mama looked up and gave Coralie a chiding eye.

Coralie huffed as she picked up her leather bound copy of *Pride and Prejudice*. Her eyes wandered over the words as she tried to justify why she wasn't writing to Joe.

He left us. He's selfish. Why should I?

The legs on Isabelle's chair screeched against the floor as the little girl flew to her mother and thrust her precious drawing in her face. "Look, Mama!"

Coralie watched over her book as Mama beamed at the drawing. "Oh, Izzy, Joe will just adore it! Now why don't you draw one for Lucas? I have something to send him, and we can include your picture in the envelope."

Isabelle skipped back to her seat and started another drawing while Coralie shook her head in disgust. "You're sending something to Lucas, Mama? Why?"

Mama lifted her head up slowly and set her eyes on Coralie. "He's my nephew and your cousin, Coralie. We can at least send him a letter."

Coralie inwardly groaned. It was all because of Lucas that she couldn't have the new dress she was so looking forward to having. Mama had promised her the dress

83

because Coralie had waited so patiently until there was a little extra money for pleasures. There wasn't any extra money now, not after what Lucas had done. Coralie was more upset than ever at her cousin.

"Well, I won't," Coralie grumbled. "I'd rather not be related to him."

"Because of that remark you *will* write him a nice note!"

"What?" Coralie slammed her book shut. "But Mama–"

"Right now."

Coralie angrily snatched a sheet of paper and picked up a pen with annoyance.

Dear Lucas Holmes,

Mama's making me write to you, even after you stole from us and made our lives extremely miserable.

Coralie Roberts

She folded the paper carelessly and stuffed it in an envelope.

"I have a very special letter for Lucas, along with the drawing from Isabelle, so please take them to the store and put them in the mail bag." Mama handed Coralie a thick envelope.

Coralie marched out of the study feeling very upset and jammed the envelope in her dress pocket as she walked across the street to the store. The shop smelled of sugary candies, fresh air and leather when Coralie walked in. Levi was prying open a window and turned to smile at her. "Good morning, Miss Roberts."

The morning sun sent shafts of light on the floor boards and illuminated Levi's light brown hair so that it appeared almost golden.

"Good morning." Coralie went behind the counter and placed her letter to Lucas and the letters for Joe in the mail bag. She fingered the letter from Mama that remained in her pocket and hesitated. She didn't know what was so important in that letter, but she was sure that Lucas was not worthy of such a treasure.

"Ah, sending a letter to Joe?" Levi joined her at the counter.

"No. To that horrid cousin of mine. Mama made me."

Levi nodded and glanced over at the sign in the window. "I hope your mother doesn't mind that I put an enlistment poster up. I'm itching to join." His blue eyes looked longingly at the poster.

Coralie rolled her eyes and marched over to the window and ripped the poster away from it. "Levi Elliott, do you want any more of our boys marching off to war? It was because of a poster like this that my brother went to that blasted war rally. And you're daft to want to join, if you ask me."

85

"Well," Levi said after a moment, his eyes twinkling mischievously. "Miss Roberts, I really should tell your mother that you used the word 'blasted'. She would think it improper, wouldn't you agree?"

"And I, Mr. Elliott, will tell her about this poster, and then she might have to fire you."

Levi grinned and took the poster from Coralie, crumpling it up and tossing it in the waste basket. "Why do you think I'm daft to want to join the army, if I may ask?"

Coralie crossed her arms and looked at him evenly. "Because you are sixteen years old and are needed here."

"Joe's sixteen, and he joined."

"Yes, I know!" Coralie pushed past him toward the door. "And I will never forgive him for leaving us, and I would never forgive you either."

Once in her bedroom she dropped the special letter for Lucas on the ground and shoved it under the bed with her foot. "Whatever's so special in that letter, Lucas Holmes, you don't deserve to read."

Joe was just finishing his breakfast and getting ready for company drills when he saw two civilians, an elderly man and woman, stroll into camp with a basket. They stood outside Lieutenant William Terry's tent and were peering into the basket as they waited for him. Joe took a long sip of coffee and watched as Lieutenant Terry came out of his tent and was handed the wicker basket. He narrowed his eyes to see against the glare that the sun was causing as it reflected off the white tents.

"What do you think that man and woman gave him?" Joe asked Oliver, who had just knocked over his mug of coffee and was trying to wipe it off his shirt.

Oliver glanced up and shrugged. "Cake or pie or somethin'."

Joe stood up and took a few steps forward to get a better look.

"I bet it's a new coat," Johnny speculated.

"Why would they put a coat in a little basket like that, Johnny? It's probably loaves of bread," Will observed.

Joe was about to predict cookies when Lieutenant Terry suddenly pulled a puppy out of the basket. Joe stared in amazement as the lieutenant took the pug-nosed pup out and held it with a smile – *a smile!* Joe had never seen Lieutenant Terry appear so pleased before. He held the puppy in his big hands and scratched behind its ears affectionately.

"What's he gonna do with a *dog?*" Oliver asked incredulously.

"Ah, he probably won't keep it," Johnny said. "Why *would* he keep it?"

Lieutenant Terry set the puppy on the ground, and Joe thought he would walk away, but he didn't. He stood

87

there, arms crossed, looking very official and important, yet watching with a little smirk as the bridle bull terrier wobbled on her legs and sniffed his boots. Lieutenant Terry noticed the boys and broke into a full fledged smile. "Haven't you boys ever seen a dog before?"

"Yes, sir," Oliver said. "Got lots at home."

Lieutenant Terry nodded. "Well then, why are you staring at it like you haven't seen the creature before in your life? Get in line for company drills."

Lieutenant Terry patted the dog on its head, then turned and walked off just as the bugle sounded. Oliver, instead of doing as he was told, took long strides over to the puppy and picked it up. It was so small that it could climb up Oliver's sleeve.

"Want to hold it, Roberts?" he asked.

Joe's eyes searched around to see if Lieutenant Terry or Captain Coulter were near. Men were coming from their tents and gathering into lines for drilling, and before he could refuse, Oliver had placed the puppy in his arms. Its soft body felt warm against Joe's chest, and its tiny nose sniffed his face.

"Hey, Roberts, I think it likes you," Will laughed as he patted the puppy's head.

The pup did seem to take a fancy to Joe which surprised him since he never had one. It continued to lick his face, and it nestled into his arms, looking quite calm and comfortable. But it didn't stay there long. A group of men had gathered and wanted a chance to hold it. Joe handed it to Johnny who was just about to hand it to Will when Captain Coulter caught them.

"What is going on here?" Captain Coulter stepped into their group, his countenance stormy. He pried the dog from Johnny's arms.

"But sir, I haven't gotten a chance to hold her!" Will complained.

Captain Coulter narrowed his eyes. "What's your name, private?

"William Story, sir."

"Private Story, this isn't a menagerie. This is the army." With that, he turned on his heels and marched off, the puppy buried in his big arms.

Will made a face as the captain walked away. "I'll betcha *he* just wanted to hold the puppy without waiting for his turn."

Chapter Ten

"A pure love of my country, and of the principles I have often advocated before the people, and the name of honor, that I love more than I fear death, have called upon me, and I have obeyed."
– Union Major Sullivan Ballou

Men, this little puppy here has become accustomed to Reveille and responds to it, but you soldiers are still grumbling and dragging yourselves out of bed. Take a lesson from the pup," Captain Coulter shouted a few weeks later at company drills.

Lucas yawned as exhaustion swept over him, and he blinked a few times to regain his vision.

Drills – mornin', noon and night. Ain't right to put a fellow through so much. When do I get to fight them Rebs?

Sallie trotted over to him and sat by his feet, glancing up now and then with her big round eyes.

"Get outta here," Lucas carped at her.

Sallie didn't move. It appeared that Lucas was her soldier pick of the day.

"Right shoulder shift! Double quick – march!" the captain commanded.

Lucas' arms and legs couldn't take it any longer. He was tired and detested drilling more than anything. He stopped and stepped out of line. "Sir, let's stop this foolishness. We've been doin' it for hours on end, and I think I speak for everyone when I say, this is balderdash!" Lucas smiled to himself for his bravery, and he looked around at the boys. Some of them stared in awe while others chuckled. Others didn't even move a muscle.

Captain Coulter whipped his head around and cried out, "Company halt!" He strode over until he was just inches from Lucas, his eyes like flames as they burned into him. He never turned his glare from Lucas as he called a corporal over. "Corporal, take this boy out and drill the heck out of him."

Lucas' eyes widened. "Who do you think you are?" he spat. "I joined the army to fight Rebs, not to obey the commands of some fool!"

Lucas felt the corporal grab his arm, and he was dragged to an empty spot of land behind the tents where he was given a knapsack full of bricks.

"Put it on your back, private," the corporal snapped.

Lucas lifted the knapsack and felt his arms burn with pain. "I don't think this is what Captain Coulter had in mind," Lucas said as he pulled it over his shoulders.

"He told me to drill you. He didn't say how. Now walk."

Lucas heaved as the heaviness weighed down upon him. He didn't falter; he wouldn't allow himself to.

"Walk faster."

Lucas lowered his head and marched on, all the while thinking what a lousy idea it was to join the army.

Lucas couldn't quite believe that he got a letter. He sat behind his tent the next day, his shoulders and back aching as he flipped the white envelope over in his hands. It was certainly addressed to him and in the corner was his cousin Coralie's name.

Why on earth is she writin' to me? he wondered bitterly.

He was almost scared to open it, for this was so unlike Coralie to make any kind of reference towards his existence. Lucas looked over his shoulder at Joe who sat near the fire, sipping coffee and reading the three letters he had received from home. He looked happy.

Lucas sighed and finally ripped the envelope open and yanked the letter out, unfolding it with suspicion. Coralie's handwriting was tiny and neat, like her, but the words were cold.

Dear Lucas Holmes,

Mama's making me write to you, even after you stole from us and made our lives extremely miserable.

Coralie Roberts

Lucas' heart fell a little, but he wouldn't allow himself to dwell on such a feeling as that. He wedged the letter back into its envelope, stood up and tossed it in the fire. He folded his arms and watched as the flames licked the envelope up. Soon it was a pile of ashes.

Should have known it wouldn't have an inch of goodwill in it, he thought to himself. *Coralie despises me, and that's just as well, for I don't feel very kindly toward her either.*

His eyes bore into Joe.

Joe glanced up. "Did you get a letter?" he asked.

Lucas ground the heel of his boot into the dirt and glowered at his cousin. "Yes, from your *charmin'* little sister."

"Oh." Joe stared down at a drawing on his lap from Isabelle. "Mama wrote to me and said she enclosed a very special letter in the envelope that Coralie's sent you along with a drawin' from Izzy. She said to make sure you read it."

"There wasn't another letter in there. Only one." Lucas inwardly wished that other letter had been enclosed, for it piqued his interest.

"What did Coralie say to you in the letter?" Joe asked.

Lucas shook his head and kicked a twig into the fire. "Your sister is a little imp." He looked up to see Joe's expression and was satisfied to see his jaw clench and his eyes flash.

"You take that back right now."

"Or what?"

Joe gave Lucas a dark scowl. "My sister took the time to write you a friendly little note. Be grateful she did because there ain't another soul in this whole country who would."

June 1861

Dear Mama, Coralie and Izzy,

I have a little more to tell you than I did in my last letter. I've done some things other than drill. Our company was sent to guard the Pittsburg, Wilmington and Baltimore railroad at the end of May in Elkton, Maryland. Nothin' much to say about that only that we finally got some uniforms. They didn't give us any coats though, but that's all right with me at the moment. It's too hot for that.

We spent all our time standing in the wide open with the sun beating down on us and practically buried in dust. Lordy, I was glad when evening came and the air was at last bearable. Nothing happened to our company, but I heard that one of the men in Company K was killed by accidental gun shot from a comrade.

It feels like we've been tossed around all over the place. The 1st Delaware relieved us finally on a hot day in June, but then we were attached to Negley's 5th brigade, 2nd Division in General Robert Patterson's army, then transferred to Abercrombie's 6th brigade. We then moved on to Williamsport, Maryland and that's where we are now. All this moving around is making my head spin, but I ain't complaining. I like the army, so don't you worry about me, you hear?

I guess I didn't tell you about Sallie, did I? Sallie is our dog mascot and she's familiar with the drum and bugle calls. She climbs into our tent in the morning to lick our faces and wake us up. She picks a different soldier each day to stand next to at roll call.

I'll write more later. Hopefully I'll have something more exciting to write about.

Yours affectionately,

Joe

Chapter Eleven

"I advise you, and as strongly as ever, to not come to war.
I tell you you will repent if you do, I do believe.
You have no idea of what it is to be a soldier."
- Joseph Boyd, a Confederate Private in a letter to his brother

Virginia, July 1861

What time is it?" Joe growled, sitting up in the pup tent he shared with Will. The July air was heavy and scorching, but the tents allowed breezes to cool the soldiers off. Joe wiped the sweat from his brow with the back of his sleeve. Will crawled out of the tent as the bugle called *First Call*.

"Stuff a sock in that bugle, would you?" Joe yelled as he tried to breathe normally amidst the muggy air. Will started singing along to the bugle call, "Darn them stinking rotten little bu-glers!"

The bugle now played *Attention* as Joe stepped out of the tent. The sky was pitch black, and only a few stars were visible through the leafy trees that swayed in a slight breeze. Joe welcomed it with relief as it cooled his hot, tired frame.

"Attention, attention, attention to all. You'd best be heeding this bugler's call!" Will sang. His voice was still crackly from having just woken up.

Joe glared at him. He sounded far too cheerful after being called to attention in the middle of the night. "Do you have a ditty for every bugle call?"

Will nodded. "It's the only way to remember all them calls, Roberts!"

Now *The Assembly* filled the air and, just like Joe expected, Will sang a little jingle to that, too. "We are the strongest men in the who-ole wide world!"

Joe wasn't the only one in a foul mood. Everyone around Will was yelling at him to pipe down as they packed up their tents and belongings. Next call was *Forward March*, and before he knew what was happening, they were marching into the night. Joe's arms and legs felt heavy, but he trudged on as Will marched beside him, singing another song that caused Joe to grit his teeth in annoyance.

"Swing your leggies, swing your leggies, swing your little leggies, swing your leggies, swing your leggies swing 'em really fast."

"Shut up, Story!" Joe hissed at him. "It's bad enough havin' to march in the dark, half awake, without you singin' on top of that."

They paraded on and on until reaching the edge of the Potomac River. Moon beams laced through the trees and sent streaks of light onto the dark water.

Now what?

Joe looked around as a shout was given from Colonel Coulter. "Company halt!"

They stood there in the dark, unsure of what was happening for a long moment. Then the sound of splashing water brought Joe's attention to the river in front of them. The men were starting to ford through the murky water. When Joe plunged in, the weight of the water pulled him down but still he went on. There was a whole group of men behind him, and he'd get trampled if he didn't keep up. He unbuckled his cartridge box, lifting it and his gun above his head.

"Who do those fools think they are, wakin' us up in the middle of the night to go swimmin'?" Joe could hear Lucas' voice somewhere behind them.

They were just reaching the other side of the river – which was the state of Virginia – when Joe's ears exploded. A surge of panic rushed through his veins as bullets flew at them from the dark woods. Someone up ahead shouted, "Reb scouts!"

The bugler called *To The Colors*, and Joe turned to Will whose eyes glinted in the moonlight. "Don't you have a song for that one, Story?" he jested grimly.

He shook his head and stared at him. "No, Roberts. It means prepare for battle, and right now I don't have much time or heart for singing."

Joe hadn't paid attention to the bugle calls as he should have. He stared at Will. "Prepare for battle? Right now?"

Will didn't answer him. He was shouldering his gun and preparing for the signal to fire. Joe looked at the land before them and glimpsed the butternut color of Reb uniforms upon horses that were galloping out of the woods.

"Commence firing!" came the order.

An outbreak of guns enclosed the area around Joe, and his throat went dry. He lifted his gun, but his arms were shaking and he could hear Will whispering along with the bugle, "One two three four, one-and-two-and-three-and-fire," then his gun sent out a screaming bullet.

"They're running off," Will shouted with a little laugh in his voice. "Cowards!"

Joe glanced up while he was loading his gun and saw the horses disappear into the dark shadows of the Virginia woods. He took a deep breath.

So, was that it? Can we go back to our camp now?

"Forward, march!" came his answer.

Joe's feet were growing sore, and his stomach rumbled. Food would have been deeply appreciated at that moment, along with a good nights sleep. The 11th

Pennsylvania was marching through enemy country. Joe's eyes were fixed on the dark woods that surrounded them, but no Rebs were spotted. The grey sky was starting to lighten with shades of pink as dawn approached. They were allowed to stop at a stream to fill their canteens along the way. Joe cupped his hands in the water and splashed it onto his raw, tired face, taking a long drink before getting back in line.

"Wait! Wait up!"

Joe turned and saw Oliver come running toward the regiment. He was soaked from head to toe and his uniform clung to him as water dripped down from his hair.

"Willyard, what happened to you?" Joe asked as Oliver slipped in beside him in the march.

"I...well I...I slipped into the stream," Oliver said, reddening. "Hold my rifle for a minute, would you?" He twisted his hat like a dish cloth, and a puddle of water formed at his feet. Once it had been adequately wrung, he took his rifle back.

"You accidentally slipped, Willyard?" Joe teased. "I can hardly believe that."

"Ha ha. You're so witty, Roberts," Oliver said sarcastically, resentment in his voice.

"I was only teasin' you, Willyard. Lighten up."

The regiment formed to the right of the road, along the edge of the woods. Heavy firing was soon heard, roaring and thundering like a devouring beast. Joe swallowed hard and tried to remain calm as his heart pounded against his ribs. They were ordered to form a line of battle on the right of the 1st Wisconsin.

Joe didn't see any Rebs, but he could hear their wild 'Rebel yell.' His head rattled as he and his comrades began firing at the white smoke.

The bugle sounded an order to cease firing as Colonel Coulter yelled, "Don't shoot until you see your targets!"

Just then the Union artillery let out an explosion of shells upon a barn up ahead. The building was swallowed by consuming flames, and Rebs darted out like insects being driven from their homes by a heavy boot. Now they could see their enemy, and the command came to commence firing.

Joe had once been eager to face the Rebs, but now horror and despair had a hold of him and wouldn't let go. His hands suddenly numbed, and his eyesight went foggy.

Pull yourself together. Just load your gun and fire!

Joe wasn't yet very fast at loading a gun, and his hands trembled which made things even more difficult. He repeated the nine steps in his head as he snatched the paper cartridge from his pocket and savagely ripped it open with his teeth, spitting it to the side. He then poured the black powder into the barrel as the sounds of firing wrapped around him.

I have to hurry. Hurry, Joe. Hurry!

The commotion of cannons, bullets and screaming formed a lump in his stomach. This wasn't how he imagined war. The air smelled of thick sulfur as the wails of the wounded sent him shaking even more.

Joe placed the bullet in the muzzle and rammed it down. Then he grabbed his percussion caps. Placing the cap on the cone, Joe cocked the gun, aimed, and fired. He was reloading his gun when he heard the deadly squeal of a bullet as it knocked the cap off his head.

"Roberts, are you okay?" Johnny crawled over to Joe.

"I'm fine." Joe fired into the smoke, unsure of where it would land.

"Don't worry, Roberts. We're gonna win this battle," Johnny fired, then turned back to him. "I know it."

The firing continued. It seemed as if it would never end until finally the sound of the Rebs' guns started to thin out. They were slowly falling back as orders were given for companies A, B, and C of the 11th Pennsylvania to outflank the retreating enemy. Joe stood there for a moment and beheld the fields as the burnt wheat blew in the wind, charred and black. He could see the white farmhouse beyond them and felt dread for the family living there. The bodies of dead and wounded soldiers stained the ground.

So this is what war is like? I had no idea.

Chapter Twelve

"Do your duty in all things. You cannot do more,
you should never wish to do less."
— Robert E. Lee

*L*ucas, *stop this foolishness and come home,"* Uncle Charles' voice flooded Lucas' dream, followed by a brawl with three drunken men and the sight of his uncle dead upon the pavement.

Sweat dripped down Lucas' face, and he sat up with a start. He was breathing hard, and he was relieved to see that no one was awake in camp.

The dreams and visions were getting worse. He had thought joining the army would be enough of a distraction, but it wasn't. Now the dreams came more frequently and more vivid each time.

He had abandoned his tent that was hardly big enough for himself, let alone two or three soldiers, and had camped out under the summer night sky. He shivered, sank down on the prickly grass and laid on his back again, gazing up at the stars. They made the world seem peaceful and pleasant, but Lucas knew better than that. The world was cold. And no one cared.

"Couldn't sleep either?"

Lucas sat up on his elbows and found Joe walking toward him. He rolled his eyes. "Go back to bed, Joe."

"I was thinkin' of home. I started re-readin' the letters I got last week and I forgot to show you this picture that Isabelle drew for me." He handed Lucas a thin piece of paper.

Lucas took it and glanced down at the stick figures. One had curly hair with the name "Joe" written over it; next to him stood Coralie and Isabelle, and then Lucas, only Isabelle spelled his name "Luukus" and the figure she had drawn of him was less than flattering. He had a horrible frown on his face, sloppy hair and hands twice as big as Joe's.

"Well, ain't that nice?" Lucas mocked, shoving the paper back at Joe.

Joe was chuckling as he folded the paper. "Great picture, ain't it? It looks just like you!"

Lucas shook his head at Joe. "Did you really have to get up in the middle of the night to show me a stupid drawin'?"

Joe straightened, his laughter vanishing. "It ain't stupid, Lucas. Izzy made this for me."

"Yes, for you! Now leave me alone!"

"Fine. I just saw that you were awake, so I thought I'd show you. Goodnight."

Lucas said nothing and watched as his cousin sauntered away. Joe was nearly as tall as Lucas now, which was infuriating.

Why was I so stupid? I should have enlisted in a regiment somewhere else. I can't stand Joe. I can't stand him!

Dear Mama, Coralie and Izzy,

Our regiment got itself the nickname "Bloody Eleventh" because of our fighting at the Battle of Falling Waters in Virginia. Nice nickname, ain't it? In case you're wondering about Sallie, she stayed at camp during the fight. She's still just a pup and would have gotten trampled by the men and artillery since she's so small. I'm mighty proud of my regiment. Right now I'm sitting by a snapping fire in Martinsburg, Virginia. We've occupied the town right outside of where the Battle of Falling Waters took place. Sallie's sitting at my feet, sighing contently after a meal. Right now the campfires are lit, everyone's talking and at least three different patriotic songs are being sung. It's really quite nice.

Martinsburg is a mixture of Southern sympathizers and Union sympathizers. Why, just a few days ago a soldier (not from our regiment) was shot in town by a young lady named Belle Boyd (a southern sympathizer, I might add) for insulting her mother. I don't think she had to go and shoot the fellow! He could have been put in the sweat box or given another punishment that would make him think twice.

But most of the townsfolk are for the Union cause and our regiment has been behaving ourselves wonderfully, as reported by many people in the few days that we've been here. We're a good group of soldiers, if I may say so!

Yours always,

Joe

The 11th Pennsylvania crowded around a wooden platform in the town square of Martinsburg, Virginia. A ceremony was about to begin in their honor, and the soldiers stood in the July sun, eager for it to begin. Harsh sunlight sent streaks of light on everything in view, and Joe would have been fried alive if it weren't for the leafy tree that he stood beneath. He took a deep breath of fresh air and felt proud of himself. Here he was, already a veteran of sorts, and here were hundreds of loyal citizens gathering around to present him and his regiment with gifts while a band played stirring tunes. Joe found himself singing along.

"So you *can* sing, Roberts!" Will said as the song ended.

Joe shrugged and leaned against his rifle. "I was only movin' my lips, Story." But Joe laughed because he had been singing his heart out, and it felt good to do so.

"Hush up," Johnny whispered to them from behind. "The ceremony is about to begin."

On the gazebo, fifteen young ladies held a woolen flag, each grasping a fold of it. One of the young ladies stepped forward, and the crowd silenced to listen. "Our brave soldiers of the 11th Pennsylvania. You helped save us from the dreaded Rebs, and for that, we are utterly grateful. The young ladies of this town have made your regiment this flag to take on your further services. May God bless you, preserve your health and lead you honorably and triumphantly through this contest."

The stillness erupted into clapping as the young lady took the flag from her friends, walked down from the platform and presented it to the colonel of their regiment, Phaon Jarrett. The band played *Stand Up For Uncle Sam* as the colonel held it up for the boys to admire. Joe hooted as pride for his country swelled in his heart.

They now had a regimental flag.

Joe was sick to his stomach after a long march in the brutal sun. His legs felt wobbly, and his sunburnt face was sore. He frowned at his ration of hardtack and coffee for supper. It wasn't much, but he was too hungry to complain. As he crumbled the stale bit of the foul tasting cracker into his coffee, he reminded himself that he really ought to send Coralie a piece of hardtack, just so she could feel sorry for what he had to eat most days.

Joe lifted the mug to his lips when his stomach gave a jolt. Weevils floated in the cup, breaking loose from the hardtack. Joe threw the mug down and ran for the woods where he heaved up his breakfast and dinner, which had both been hardtack.

"You okay?" Will asked when Joe returned, clutching his stomach and feeling infirmed. Will was frying his hardtack over the fire, and he gave Joe a sympathetic look. "You're not okay, Roberts. You look sick as a dog."

Joe moaned, sinking to the ground and feeling as if
he might cry while listening to Johnny sing.

Let us pause in life's pleasures and
    count its many tears,
While we all sup sorrow with the poor;
There's a song that will linger forever in our ears;
Oh, hard times come again no more.

'Tis the song, the sigh of the weary,
Hard times, hard times, come again no more.
Many days you have lingered around my cabin door;
Oh, hard times come again no more.

Johnny was the serious and pensive one of the Story
brothers, and that fact was once more confirmed as Will
snickered and said, "I heard that song before, only with
different lyrics. Listen to this." He started to sing, only not
as soft and sentimentally as his brother.

Let us close our game of poker,
    take our tin cups in hand,
While we gather round the cook's tent door.
Where dried mummies of hard crackers
    are given to each man;
Oh, hard crackers come again no more!

'Tis the song and the sigh of the hungry,
Hard crackers, hard crackers, come again no more!
Many days have you lingered upon
    our stomachs sore,
Oh, hard crackers come again no more.

Joe couldn't help but laugh as Will ended his song and took a hearty bite of his hardtack, still singing, "Oh, hard crackers come again no more!"

Chapter Thirteen

*"This, soldiers, be your future fate: Your fame that longest shall
endure, 'Tis noble thus to save a State,
but nobler still to keep it pure."
— Bayard Taylor*

Genevieve sat down in the parlor with a cup of tea and
the shirts that she was sewing for Joe and Lucas. She
gazed at Coralie who was sitting across from her, knitting.
Isabelle was playing in the middle of the floor with her
dolls, and it was the ideal time for her sewing projects. But
Genevieve couldn't stay focused.

"Coralie?" She broke the silence, and Coralie tore her
eyes away from her knitting.

"Yes, Mama?"

"Won't you go over to the store and see if there's a
letter from Joe or Lucas? We haven't heard from them in
ages." She was more concerned about Lucas, for she
hadn't received any word from him. She was certain he
would write after receiving that wonderful letter from his
mother.

"I went over this morning for you, Mama,
remember?" Coralie said.

"Oh, yes." Genevieve looked down at the shirts on her lap and felt her heart tighten. "I wonder why Lucas hasn't written," she said aloud.

Coralie didn't look up. She continued to knit as she gripped her needles tighter.

"You did send the letter I gave you, didn't you, Coralie?"

Coralie slowly lifted her eyes, and Genevieve wondered why she looked so pale all of a sudden. "I sent the letter *I* wrote him, Mama."

"Yes, but did you send the letter that I specifically asked of you?"

The parlor door creaked open as she was speaking, and Levi Elliott stood in the doorway, hat in his hands. Genevieve smiled at him and motioned for him to come in.

"I closed the store, Mrs. Roberts. Everything's locked up," Levi said respectfully.

"Thank you, Levi." Genevieve looked at the young boy and images of Joe flashed through her mind. "Won't you stay and have supper with us?"

Levi smiled but shook his head, like he always did when she asked him that question. She knew his answer by memory. "Thank you, ma'am, but my mama wants us younger boys home for meals. She gets lonesome without us."

Genevieve nodded. "Yes, I understand that." She watched as he left and was so absorbed in her thoughts of

Joe and days gone by that she didn't ask any more questions of Coralie.

End of July 1861

Dear Mama, Coralie and Izzy,

I wish you could see what Harpers Ferry looks like. We got here not long ago along with General Robert Patterson's army to occupy the town. It's grand! After marching in the brutal sun and living off hardtack (which I've enclosed for you to try. Make sure there ain't no weevils in it before you take a bite), I was in a foul mood, but even I had to admit that Harpers Ferry was mighty pretty looking. The Blue Ridge Mountains are thick with leaves and surround a little town where there are brick houses and roads that curve in and out of the mountains.

Our regiment has been mustered out of our ninety day service, but before you get all excited and think I'm done with the army, I'm not. First of all, after we were mustered out, the old man, General Robert Patterson, said something awfully nice to us 11th PA men. Here's what he said:

"It gives the commanding general great satisfaction to say that the conduct of this regiment has merited its highest approbation. It had the fortune to be in the advance at Falling Waters, where the steadiness and gallantry of both the officers and men came under personal observation. They have well merited his thanks."

Wasn't that nice? Well, after that the General asked all the regiments under his command to remain a week or so until there were reinforcements to take our place. Our regiment was called and we all stood in front of the General and his staff to make our decision. He said, "Those who are willing to stay, bring rifle to shoulder." So when he said, "Shoulder arms!" all our rifles went up! You should have seen the look on General Patterson's face!Next thing he said was, "With you, my brave Blue Jackets, I can hold the place alone."

Our regiment will be organizing for three years of service now, as it's evident that the war won't be over as soon as we all thought. I won't be comin' home, not now anyway. I'm a soldier in the 11th Pennsylvania, and right proud to say so.

Your loving son and brother,

Joe

Chapter Fourteen

"Captain, my religious belief teaches me to feel as safe in battle as in bed. God has fixed the time for my death. I do not concern myself about that, but to be always ready, no matter when it may overtake me. Captain, that is the way all men should live, and then all would be equally brave."
— Stonewall Jackson

June 1863

She's fifteen years old and still doesn't know how to clean up after herself," Genevieve groaned as she stepped into Coralie's bedroom. Coralie was spending more time working in the store lately with Levi and less time minding to her chores and picking up after herself. Genevieve held a pile of books in her arms that had been scattered throughout the house. She set them on Coralie's dressing table which induced a cloud of dust to dance through the air.

Horrified, Genevieve ran a finger along the surface of the table, and it turned black with dust and filth. The windows were so smudged she could barely see out of them; her quilt was wrinkled from a half hearted making that morning, and Genevieve didn't even want to look underneath the bed. She shook her head in disgust and went to her bedroom, changed into a work dress, snatched the broom, dustpan and a cloth and headed for Coralie's room like a soldier going into battle.

The surfaces were quickly wiped clean, and the floor was looking better, though it did need a good scrubbing. She wiped the windows and opened them to let in fresh air, and then she hesitated as she glanced at the bed. She gave it a shove against the wall to see what hid beneath it. Dust lay in clumps, mingled with books and half a dozen papers.

"She's just like her brother. Doesn't care about a few dust bunnies or dirty windows," she muttered.

Genevieve leaned over and picked up a white envelope. She started to throw it on the bed with everything else when she saw familiar handwriting on the front. Her heart leapt to her throat, and her breathing quickened. This was the letter from her sister. She had told Coralie to send it to Lucas two years ago. Her surprise quickly vanished, replaced by disappointment and confusion.

How could she hide this? Why didn't she send it to him?

For a moment, she could hardly move. Hot tears stung her eyes as she held the precious letter in her hands. Then she made up her mind to find Coralie and confront her. Ignoring her disheveled state, Genevieve marched across the road to the store. With the envelope in her hands and a pain in her heart, she shoved open the door.

Coralie was sweeping the floors while laughing at something Levi said. Over the past two years, Genevieve had sensed that Coralie and Levi were growing fond of each other.

"Good morning, Mrs. Roberts," Levi said. He had grown much taller and his boyish face had gradually turned into a man's. It caused an ache in her heart when she looked at him, for she was reminded of Joe. She was very much in awe that Levi hadn't run off to the join the army yet.

"Good morning, Levi," she said, her tone less friendly than her usual greetings. "Coralie, come here."

Coralie looked confused, but she set down her broom and walked across the store to stand before her mama. Her eyes looked so much like her father's.

"Yes, Mama?"

"I found this while cleaning your room." Genevieve's voice broke as she held out the envelope. Coralie's rosy face drained of color so fast that she looked rather ill. "Why did you hide it? Why didn't you send it to Lucas?"

"Mama, I–"

"This letter is very important!" Genevieve's voice was growing stronger and she suddenly realized that she was shouting. "I trusted you to send it! I don't understand why you didn't, Coralie!"

Coralie's pale face quickly regained color, and her eyes flashed with anger. "I didn't send it because I knew you thought it was special, and Lucas doesn't deserve to read it. He only deserves that spiteful letter I sent him!"

Genevieve couldn't believe her ears, and she felt a tear running down her cheek. "There are many good and wonderful things which we don't deserve. Thank God that He gives us grace and not what we *truly* deserve. 'Blessed are the merciful, for they will be shown mercy.' Aren't we all horribly flawed, not just your cousin?"

Coralie stared down at her feet, but she didn't look remorseful or even ashamed. She looked bitter.

"I'm disappointed, Coralie. More than I can say. Go to the house this moment."

Coralie marched out of the store, and the door slammed shut behind her. The store fell silent. Genevieve took a deep breath, pushed her hair back and walked to the counter where she found a fresh envelope. She slipped the special letter inside and addressed it to the last place Joe had written from.

Lord, please let it get to him. Please don't let it be too late.

"Are you in a heap of trouble for not sending the letter?" Levi asked Coralie as she sat behind the counter at the store the next day.

"Of course," she scowled. "I can't go to the Volunteer Aid Society Gala, nor the fair to raise money for the war. I can't go to the ladies sewing circle meeting –

or anything for that matter." She sighed, feeling great pity for herself. "It's not fair."

"And you think it was right not to send the letter?" Levi leaned against the counter and raised a brow.

"Yes. Lucas is awful and shouldn't be rewarded with nice letters." Coralie sat up straight, fully believing her reasoning.

Levi shrugged and stepped away from the counter, shoving his hands in his pockets. "Coralie, I have something I want to tell you."

Coralie gazed down at her pale, smooth hands and waited for him to go on. There was a long silence, and she looked up. "What, Levi?"

"I won't be working here anymore."

Coralie's skin grew cold, and she knew what Levi was going to say next. But she wouldn't let him. She jumped up. "Oh, I see," she said quickly. "You're getting a new job? Well, you better come and visit me, for we have grown to be such good friends, haven't we?" She was nervously working around the store now, dusting, wiping and setting things in order. Coralie's throat tightened as Levi spoke the inevitable next words.

"I'm joining the army."

Those few simple words felt like stones in Coralie's stomach. She breathed in and turned away from him to stare at the wall. Emotions flooded her. "You're just like Joe, leaving without anyone to help us. And after I've grown so fond of you! I hate this war! It was only supposed to last three months. Now look! I haven't seen Joe in two years and I shan't see you in just as long. You'll die. I know it." She was trembling.

"Coralie, I'm very fond of you, too," Levi said softly. He strode toward her and took her hands in his. "So I hope you'll marry me when I come back." He looked into her eyes. "Will you?"

Coralie stared at him in shock. She felt a horrible, foreboding feeling rise in her and slowly let go of his hands. "You're going to war, Levi. You'll die and leave me, and then what shall I do?"

"That isn't a very hopeful thought to dwell on, Coralie. You seem to think I'll die right off."

Coralie blinked away tears as she ran a hand over the patterned fabric on the table near the front of the store. "It's not fair, Levi. Why can't life be what it was before the war?"

"Things will get better," he smiled, but Coralie sensed fear in his tone.

"I'm not so sure about that anymore."

Chapter Fifteen

"Sir, my concern is not whether God is on our side; my greatest concern is to be on God's side, for God is always right."
— Abraham Lincoln

June 1863

Lucas sat near the fire, devouring a cup of weevil infested hardtack and coffee for supper. He was tired, and his bones ached, making him feel like an old man. He had just turned twenty while shooting Rebs at the Battle of Fredericksburg.

The past two years had proved to be more challenging than he anticipated. He hadn't been able to ward of the hateful memories of the past, and the war proved to be anything but the escape he hoped it would be.

Music drifted in the night air. It was a melancholy song that caused Lucas to stop thinking and just listen with a heavy heart.

We're tenting tonight on the old camp ground

Give us a song to cheer

Our weary hearts, a song of home

And friends we love so dear

Many are the hearts that are weary tonight
Wishing for the war to cease
Many are the hearts that are looking for the right
To see the dawn of peace
Tenting tonight, tenting tonight,
    tenting on the old camp ground

We've been tenting tonight on the old camp ground
Thinking of days gone by
Of the loved ones at home that gave us the hand
And the tear that said "Goodbye"

We are tired of war on the old camp ground
Many are dead and gone
Of the brave and true who've left their homes
Others been wounded long

We've been fighting today on the old camp ground
Many are lying near
Some are dead and some are dying
Many are in tears

He shook his head, and his chest compressed.

Silly, for a song to make me want to cry. Don't cry, you fool.

He managed to keep his tears in check and breathed heavily as he kicked a hot stick back into the fire. He was a wreck. Every night he found himself dreaming or thinking of his father's cruel words, or his uncle's death. Every day something happened to make him think of his foolish mistakes.

Lucas scratched the side of his face where a beard was growing in. He had caught his reflection in the river while filling up his canteen earlier that day and nearly lost his breath. He thought it was his father staring back at him.

"Here." Joe stalked over to Lucas and tossed him an envelope. "I got a letter from Mama today. She enclosed this and insisted that it get to you no matter what."

Lucas held the thick envelope in his hands skeptically. "Another charmin' letter from Coralie? No, it must be a flatterin' drawin' from Isabelle."

"How should I know?" Joe huffed as he turned and walked off. He had become even more arrogant than ever in last two years and hardly said a word to Lucas unless he had to. This suited Lucas just fine. He didn't fancy talking to Joe either.

It's probably just a note from Aunt Genevieve hopin' that I'm havin' a good time or some such nonsense.

The letter was rather thick which made him curious. He flipped it over and found that it said *Genevieve Roberts* where his name should have been. His eyes fell on the return address, and he gasped. It was his mother's name.

Caroline Holmes.

He looked up, confused. Then he glanced back down again.

What's going on? Is this Joe's idea of a joke?

Lucas nearly tossed the letter aside, but something made him hold onto it. He stood up and took a walk away from the fire and the music as he tore open the envelope. With shaking hands, he retrieved the letter and soaked in the scent of old paper mixed with a fading lavender perfume. "1844" was written in the corner.

Dearest sister,

I'm aching to see you. You must come visit us as soon as you can spare the time. You haven't met my darling baby boy, Lucas, yet and he must meet his Aunt Genevieve, or I'll be cross with you!

Oh, Genevieve, I'm so happy! I can't contain my joy and so I must write to you about my dear child. He's sixteen months old now with wild brown hair like mine, beautiful, darling brown eyes and two dimples on his chubby cheeks. When I see him, my heart feels so full of love that I just throw my arms around his little body and hug him for as long as he allows me!

Lucas is the sweetest boy. He gives me kisses and smiles that melt my heart. Dear sister, you will understand how it is when you have a child, so for now, please let me continue to talk about my boy.

126

I have so many dreams and prayers for him. But not the kind people tend to think parents might be dreaming for their children. I don't care if he becomes a doctor, a lawyer, musician or some such thing. I would not pressure him into becoming what I want him to become, for God is in control of his future and I shall not interfere with His plans. I only pray that he will be good and Godly, loyal and chivalrous. I want to raise him right, Genevieve. I want him to be kind toward others, respectful and well mannered and an all around gentleman. I must confess, when I look at his innocent face, I can't imagine he would be anything but good. I still pray to God that he will be a good boy, a fine young man and a wise old man.

At this moment, he's sitting on the floor with wooden blocks and babbling on about "up" and "down"! Genevieve, he's such a blessing from heaven, and I pray he will be a blessing to others. Come visit us soon, dear sister.

Your loving sister,

Caroline

Lucas didn't realize a tear had slid down his face. He stood there with blurred eyes as the tears kept coming. His hands shook uncontrollably. His eyes darted back to a passage in the letter that had induced the tear, and he read it again through his pain.

I only pray that he will be good and Godly, loyal and chivalrous. I want to raise him right, Genevieve. I want him to be kind toward others, respectful and well mannered and an all around gentleman. I must confess, when I look at his innocent face, I can't imagine he would be anything but good. I still pray to God that he will be a good boy, a fine young man and a wise old man.

127

He shook his head at those words.

I can't claim even one of those virtues.

He looked into the dark sky as the honesty stung his heart. His mother had such hopes and dreams for his future. She had truly loved him. A prayer started to burn in his soul as all the years of hatred and guilt pressed upon him.

"Oh, God, can you possibly forgive me? I don't know if I can change. Please, help me."

Chapter Sixteen

Though Satan should buffet, though trials should come,
Let this blest assurance control,
That Christ has regarded my helpless estate,
And hath shed His own blood for my soul.

My sin, oh, the bliss of this glorious thought!
My sin, not in part but the whole,
Is nailed to the cross, and I bear it no more,
Praise the Lord, praise the Lord, O my soul!

– Horatio Spafford

July 1863

Coralie, please come sit with me," Mama said as Coralie was passing the parlor door on her way upstairs. Coralie slowly stepped in, sensing a scolding as she settled herself across from Mama on the sofa. Feeling that she was in the right, she held her chin up and stared evenly at her mother.

"It was very wrong what you did with the letter, Coralie. You told me your reasons, and I'm afraid I don't think they are good enough for what you did." Mama's voice was cold.

"But–" Coralie wanted to defend herself, but Mama continued talking.

"You have always had a bad attitude toward Lucas, and I know he is difficult at times, but he's a good boy deep inside."

Coralie couldn't help but laugh at that. "Mama, how can you say that after all he's done?"

Mama set down her sewing and stared at Coralie in such a disappointed way that Coralie's eyes fell. "I received a letter from Lucas that I'd like to read to you. Listen well, my dear:

"Dear Aunt Genevieve,

"I ain't so good at writing letters. I tried writing this letter at least ten times, but they all ended up in the fire. I read the letter you sent me from my mama. It made me think about a lot of things. I never meant to hurt you or Uncle Charles. He was a real good man and he tried so hard to help me. If it hadn't been for me, he'd still be alive. I can say right certain, ma'am, that I've never in my life felt such hellish guilt and pain.

"I never did tell you this. I didn't know how. After my mama died, my father changed. He didn't want me around no more and if I was around, I was sure to get a beating. I was lonely, so I spent most of my growing up years on the streets with my "friends". That was the only place that felt like home.

"My life ain't become something that my mama would be proud of. Or God. And I can't live with that. I've never felt forgiveness before, but God's forgiven me. I ain't sure how I know, but I know. I beg you, Aunt Genevieve, Joe, Coralie and Isabelle....please forgive me. Your humble servant, Lucas."

Coralie hadn't realized that she wasn't breathing. She stared at Mama and felt so chilled to the bone that she couldn't say anything.

"Lucas was wallowing in loneliness and guilt, Coralie. His heart turned cold. That letter I wanted you to send was written years ago by his mother and had something in it that I thought would help Lucas to turn around and start thinking of grace and forgiveness again. That's why it was so important that you send it right away, and here I found it two years later."

Coralie swallowed and nodded, feeling unbearable remorse as she hurried to the study and began a letter for her cousin, asking *him* to forgive *her*.

Gettysburg, Pennsylvania

Sallie marched alongside Joe, both dog and boy growing weary from the heat. Sallie's long tongue hung out as she panted for air, and Joe didn't feel much better. It was hard to breathe in such oppressive heat, and he longed for a good old Pennsylvania winter at the moment. He passed the time by thinking of snow and ice, sledding and chilly mornings.

"Halt!"

Joe stopped in his tracks as sweat dripped down the side of his face. They were now part of the Second Division, Second Brigade, controlled by General Robinson and General Baxter.

"Who do these Rebs think they are, coming into our home state like this?" Will said hotly. He had grown taller than Johnny, and his eyes were not quite so blue as they once had been. War had seemed to drain the spirits out of everyone.

"We're not gonna let them win, Story," Joe said, clapping a hand on his comrade's shoulder. "We can't let them win." Feeling a hand on his arm, he spun around to find Oliver appearing rather pale and ill. "Joe, might I have a sip of water from your canteen? Mine's plumb out, and there's no stream around. I'm feelin' awfully light headed from the heat."

Joe agreed and tugged the canteen off his shoulder, thrusting it toward Oliver. "Go ahead."

He watched as Oliver drank it down savagely, water dripping down his chin and soaking the collar of his uniform. He wiped his mouth with the back of his hand and gave the canteen back to Joe. "Thanks. You're a good friend, Roberts."

"Eleventh Pennsylvania and Ninety-Seventh New York!" Colonel Coulter was shouting. "By file! Right! March!"

The moments before going into battle were always the worst in Joe's life. Prayers were sent up as his heart throbbed against his heaving chest. They marched into an open clearing called Oak Ridge where the Rebs were in clear view under the scorching sun. A split second of stifling silence hung over the soldiers, then an explosion of bullets ripped through the air. The familiar stench of sulfur filled his nose. Joe tried to swallow, but found to his surprise that he couldn't.

Cannons shook the earth and rang in Joe's ears.

I hate artillery. I hate it.

Sweat dripped down from his curly hair. He ripped off his hat and stuffed it under his arm for a moment. Mournfully, he peered around at his comrades and wondered who would survive this battle...and who would not. He was about to reach for his canteen when a bullet squealed by his ear, and he thought better of it.

"Roberts, you okay?" Oliver shouted, turning to Joe. "You're awfully pale. Didn't get hit did you?" Oliver's grim countenance looked worried.

Joe shook his head. "I'm fine, Willyard. Don't worry about me."

Sallie was barking and baring her teeth at the enemy. She ran into the field and sank her teeth into a Reb's leg.

With everyone shouting at the top of their lungs, the bugle commands were lost in the constant rumble. Joe loaded his gun and shot into the smoke. He loaded and shot again. He was like a machine, just loading without his body knowing what he was doing.

"Roberts, where's Sallie?" Will yelled to him.

Joe shrugged and looked around. She must have gotten lost in the confusion. Joe kept watching for her but as the fields became wet with blood, he realized that he had no time. He was about to rip open another cartridge when he heard an agonizing scream beside him. His head whipped around, and he spotted Oliver slumped in the grass, dark blood seeping through his uniform. His hands clutched the side of his stomach, and his face was pale and contorted in torment.

"Oliver!" Joe tried shouting, but no sound escaped his mouth.

His friend was groaning. Oliver turned his trembling head toward Joe, his eyes wild. A sickening wave of terror washed over Joe as he bent to help him, but an order came to withdraw as reinforcements surged forward. As he lost sight of Oliver in a blur of blue jackets and smoke, a cold fist closed over his heart.

He knew his friend would die lying there. There was nothing he could do to save him.

His head felt dizzy as they were pushed back into the town of Gettysburg. The air was a thick sheet of bullets as they ran down the road, past homes and stores that were hastily closed and locked.

He was in a daze. He saw the terrified faces of his comrades. The grey uniform of his foes. Soldiers running, screaming, and crying out in pain. Cannons ripped through the earth. As the pulse roared in his ears, Joe barely heard the warning hum before a bullet slammed into his shoulder, feeling like a hot iron on his skin. It tore through him, dragging him down to his knees. For a moment, Joe didn't realize what had happened. Then he doubled over as nauseating pain consumed him. Soldiers ran by, paying him no mind. Joe swallowed hard as his rifle tumbled to the ground.

"Joe!"

He thought he heard Lucas through the chaotic noise, but he couldn't be sure.

Joe gasped for breath and cried out with such agony that he didn't recognize his own voice. An instant later he spotted a bearded Reb with soot and ashes covering his face charging toward him with a rifle aimed at Joe's chest.

I'm dead. I'm dead. God have mercy on me, I'm dead.

A body leapt in front of him, tackling the enemy just as the gun went off. The body rolled onto the ground, staining the street with blood as the Reb jumped up and darted off.

Joe's eyes widened, realizing who had saved his life.

"Lucas!" Joe screamed, but it was unheard in the commotion. His cousin lay before him, a bullet in his chest where it should have been in Joe's. Joe couldn't speak, but crawled over to his cousin and prayed that he was still alive. "Lucas! Oh, dear God!" Lucas' uniform was soaked in blood. His face was ashen, but he reached out and clutched Joe's arm.

"Joe," Lucas' voice was dry. "Joe, I'm sorry. I'm sorry for being so – so awful," Lucas said so softly that Joe could hardly hear him above all the death around them. "Forgive me, Joe. Please."

Joe grabbed Lucas' arm tightly, his heart splitting inside him. "No, Lucas," tears streamed down his cheeks, "*You* must forgive me."

Lucas nodded, suddenly turning deathly pale. "Run, Joe," he whispered. His body sank into the ground. His breathing stopped.

"No!" Joe shouted and shook Lucas, forgetting the pain in his arm.

"Boys, help me get Joe," came Will's voice.

Everything went still and quiet as Joe felt himself being picked up. He didn't make a sound. He couldn't. The last thing he remembered seeing was leaves, tumbling to the ground, penetrated with bullet holes.

Chapter Seventeen

'In great deeds, something abides. On great fields, something stays.
Forms change and pass; bodies disappear; but spirits linger, to
consecrate ground for the vision-place of souls... generations that
know us not and that we know not of, heart-drawn to see where and
by whom great things were suffered and done for them, shall come to
this deathless field, to ponder and dream; and lo! the shadow of a
mighty presence shall wrap them in its bosom, and the power of the
vision pass into their souls."
–Joshua Lawrence Chamberlain

Genevieve sat on the edge of her bed and gazed out the window, trying not to shed anymore tears, but they kept coming. She couldn't stop them. The casualty list from the Battle of Gettysburg had been in the paper the day before, and Lucas' name was on it. Joe was listed among the wounded. Genevieve didn't know what to do except close herself in her room to pray and weep. She knew Coralie was doing the same, for the apology letter hadn't had time to reach Lucas before he was killed.

She had finally made up her mind to go to the hospital in Gettysburg and find Joe when Mrs. Elliott knocked on the bedroom door. She had come to take care of Isabelle and cook meals while Genevieve was in mourning. "A letter for you, Genevieve," she said softly.

Genevieve tried to compose herself as she opened the door a crack. "Thank you," she murmured, then ripped open the soiled letter. It wasn't anyone's handwriting that she recognized; it was neat and very feminine.

Dear Mrs. Roberts,

I'm writing to you on behalf of your son, Private Joseph Roberts, who was wounded at Gettysburg. He is being sent home and will be unable to fight again as his left arm was amputated to save his life. He will need rest and constant care once arriving. I am only a little girl who lives here in Gettysburg and volunteered to help our boys, but I will do everything in my power to see that your son comes home swiftly and safely.

Sincerly,

Amelia Williams

Joe stood in front of his house for the first time in over two years. During the entire trip home, he had tried to soak in everything that had happened.

Why would Lucas die for me? he kept wondering, until it became an obsession in his mind. *We never got along. We were awful to each other. And then he goes and dies for me? It doesn't make any sense!*

He stared down at the place where his left arm once had been and sighed. Things would never be the same again.

Joe looked up and spotted Isabelle's nose pressed against the window. He chuckled as she came bolting out of the house, looking taller and older, and yet still with messy hair and her sweet smile. "Joe's home!" she shouted.

"Come here, little curly head!" Joe called to Isabelle, who bounded off the stairs. But she stopped short when she noticed his missing arm. Her face turned red, and she looked away nervously. His heart ached at Isabelle's hesitation.

The door slammed, and Mama came darting from the house with such a look of happiness that Joe grinned from ear to ear. She took no heed of his arm and embraced him in a loving hug. Finally, Isabelle sprang forward and swaddled her arms around his legs.

"Joe, it's so good to see you! We've missed you ever so much. You must be hungry and tired," Mama said, gazing into his eyes lovingly. "I'll fix you something to eat."

"And me, too?" Isabelle asked, skipping alongside them into the house.

"Oh, Izzy, you've already had your dinner," Mama laughed, but she gave Isabelle a thick slice of bread with butter, before setting out ham, cheese, bread, coffee and molasses cookies for Joe.

He sat at the old table that wobbled and traced the familiar marks and scratches in the wood. The house smelled and sounded just like he remembered. He took a breath of the sweet smoke coming from the fire and relished in the simple, comforting harmony of coffee bubbling, chairs screeching against the floor, the old grandfather clock ticking loudly from the parlor and Isabelle's high pitched voice as she chattered on and on.

"Your arm—" Mama said gently, after he had finished the last slice of ham and wiped his face with the back of his sleeve. "What happened, Joe?"

He swallowed and then looked down where his arm once had been. A million images, smells and sounds rushed through his brain at once. Thankfully, Mama understood his pained expression. "We'll talk about it later."

He nodded and took a long sip of sweet coffee, without fear of finding weevils in it, and then gazed around the cozy kitchen. "Where's Coralie?"

Mama sighed and wrapped her hands around a mug of coffee. She looked the same as when he left except for a weariness that showed itself around her eyes. "Coralie's deeply troubled, Joe. She had written a lovely letter for Lucas, apologizing for being so cruel in her last letter, but she sent it the day before we read his name on the casualty list. And, Levi Elliott has run off to be a soldier. It nearly broke her heart in two."

Joe's heart tugged uncomfortably, but he hid his sorrow behind his mug of coffee. He never thought the day would come when he'd wish to see his hated cousin come into the room. But now he did.

"Maybe I can talk to her," he said aloud, realizing that Mama had been staring at him as his mind wandered.

Joe supposed he looked a great deal older than she remembered.

Isabelle climbed into a chair and started to take a sip of Joe's coffee, but Mama swiftly pulled it away from her. "I think that's a good idea, Joe. She will be so pleased to see you."

Joe slowly headed up the wooden steps to the second floor of his house. How many times had he run up and down them without feeling gratitude for his home, his family, or his very life? He exhaled as he leaned against Coralie's wooden door. He heard her muffled sobs as he knocked.

"Please, leave me alone, Mama! I'm not hungry!"

Joe was momentarily taken aback. Her voice sounded different now – so grown up. He turned the knob and strolled right into the bright bedroom where Coralie was situated at her window seat, crying into her knees.

"Hi, Coralie," he said casually, as if he hadn't been away at war for two years.

Her head flew up in an instant, face raw and red from tears, and brown hair tangled as it tumbled about her shoulders. Coralie's mouth fell open and her eyes broadened.

"Joe!" She flew from the window and flung herself at him in a wild hug. "I was so worried about you! Mama said you were being sent home, but I thought it would be at least another week until you came!"

"Well, here I am, safe and sound." He smiled down at her. "Good Lord, Coralie, you've grown up. You're no longer that two braided little girl who used to follow me around."

Coralie smiled sadly and wiped the tears from her face with the back of her hands. "I wish nothing changed, Joe. Everything's just so horrible right now." It was then that she noticed his missing arm, and she swallowed and stared.

"I'm alive, Coralie," Joe said, catching her stunned expression. "And I'm thankful I made it through that mess, even if I had to lose an arm. I...I learned a lot since I've seen you."

She was quiet for a moment, then she took a wobbly breath. "I have, too." She turned and gazed out the window with a wistful look upon her rosy face. "Joe," she choked, "I'm an abominable girl." She burst into tears, causing Joe to jump in alarm.

He gently made his way toward her and set his hand on her shaking shoulder. "Hush, Coralie. You ain't an abominable girl."

She spun around with eyes pooled with tears. "I am! You don't know how bad I was, Joe."

"I see." He sank into her window seat and studied her with a little smile. "Should I take the strap to you?" he teased.

Coralie shook her head. She perched on her desk chair with an ashamed air. "Joe, I haven't been much help to Mama these past two years. I've caused her much grief, and I'm sorry for it. But I did something very bad. Mama asked me to send a special letter that she had found from Aunt Caroline to Lucas. I didn't. I sent Lucas a heartless, short letter and hid the other under my bed. I didn't think he deserved it, Joe! Two years later, Mama found it and sent it off to him. He replied with a wonderful letter asking us all to forgive him and telling of his dreadful upbringing by Uncle Simeon who paid him no heed. I was cruel toward Lucas. I should have been more understanding. I never got a chance to ask for his forgiveness."

"I didn't know that about his upbringin'," Joe started, realizing that he too should have been more understanding. He looked at his sister, saying slowly, "Coralie, if father hadn't saved Lucas, I wouldn't be sittin' here with you right now."

Coralie blew her nose with her handkerchief and stared at Joe. "What do you mean?"

"Lucas saved my life. He took a bullet for me, even after I was haughty and rude to him. I...I didn't deserve that."

Coralie stood up and grabbed Joe's hand as he turned his face away from her, trying to hide his tears. "I guess it's true what Mama once told me, Joe," she said. " 'There are many good and wonderful things which we don't deserve. Thank God that He gives us grace and not what we *truly* deserve.' "

Joe squeezed his sister's hand. "Let's not hold bitterness or cruel feelings toward anyone again. It only brings grief."

They were silent for a moment until Joe couldn't help but smile. "Now, Coralie, we have another matter to discuss." His voice was light hearted as he brushed away her tears.

"And what is that?"

Joe grinned. "Why has Levi Elliott's leavin' caused such a tear into your heart?"

Historical Note

As I was researching for this book, I came across strange facts that may sound like things I made up. The snow in May at Camp Curtin and the soldiers playing leap frog at Camp Wayne are both true. I tried to be as historically correct as possible, but sometimes historical facts are a little bizarre!

The 11th Pennsylvania participated in many engagements from 1861-1865. Besides the Battle of Gettysburg and Battle of Falling Waters (also called Hoke's Run) they were present at Cedar Mountain, Rappahannock Station, Thoroughfare Gap, Bull Run, Chantilly, South Mountain, Antietam, Fredericksburg, Chancellorsville, Mine Run, Wilderness, Spotsylvania, North Anna, Totopotomoy, Bethesda Church, Cold Harbor, Petersburg, Weldon Railroad, Dabney's Mill, Boydton Road, Five Forks, and Appomattox.

In 1890, a monument was dedicated to the 11th Pennsylvania in Gettysburg, and a speech was given by Captain Henry Piper of Company E. I've enclosed my favorite parts of the speech to share with you because I think it effectively sums up the courage, devotion, and patriotism of the 11th Pennsylvania Volunteer Regiment during the Civil War. Enjoy.

"My comrades; To have taken part on the side of the Union in the late Civil War is of much importance, and to have participated as a member of that grand old regiment, the Eleventh Pennsylvania Volunteers, may be counted an honorable distinction....

"Entering the service at the beginning, and continued to the end, participating in the first and last battles of the war, its very name became the synonym of patriotism and bravery. Early in April, 1861, the old Eleventh was organized as a three months regiment under the first call for troops by the President, and saw some practical campaigning during that period, participating in the battle of Falling Water, Virginia, which was the first infantry fight of the war...

"It was the first Pennsylvania regiment to reorganize for three years' service. On July 15th, 1861, by official order of the Secretary of War, its services as a regimental organization were formally accepted, and it again entered on a career as one of the most faithful of all faithful military organizations placed in the field by our native State in those dark and bloody days...

"The old Eleventh, the heroes of a score of bloody conflicts, breathed their native air, trod their natives vales, stretched their line of living valor along the crests of their native hills, and battled for the homes of their childhoods. Never did men more eagerly seek the field of carnage...

"The veterans of our own gallant regiment fought only as brave and determined as men can fight in defense of their homes and their country...

"Years have elapsed since these hills reverberated to the thunder of the enemy's cannon. The soil, once red with patriot blood, grows ranks with tangled grasses, or is starred with summer flowers. The eternal hills, lifting themselves toward the heavens, silenced as though the spirit of solitude sat enthroned upon their changeless summits, give no signs of the red current of battle that, twenty-seven years ago, rolled around their rocky bases….

"But the level of the eastern sky touches with softened ray the granite slabs and monumental shafts that mark the final resting places of the ashes into which has mouldered the brave hot hearts who fought, who fell, who died that the Union might be preserved. They were willing to wash out the footprints of the Rebel foe with their blood, and count it a joy to die….

"I would not if I could, forget the uncrowned and unsung hero of the knapsack and the musket. History furnishes no parallel to the gallantry of our citizen soldiers, the courage and grit of the American volunteer. The perils and hardships of the war were his. His were the lonely vigils of the picket beat, and the dangers by flood and field. Upon his brave heart and conscience lay the political destiny of this great republic. The nation placed her life in his hands. And on a hundred bloody battlefields he proved himself sublimely worthy of the trust.

"Among this unselfish host of brave, true men, none were more brave and true than the soldiers of the old Eleventh. Their bones lie on every great battlefield of the east, and the records of southern prisons show the names of some of our gallant boys, not permitted to share a soldier's death on the field of battle, but dying like some ancient martyr in love with his God and his country. To him, to the common soldier, to our dead comrades, whether here beneath this soil he sleeps, or under the softer skies of the sunny south-land, we turn in grateful, tearful remembrance. We rear these monuments to their honor and in their memory…

"But in the unborn ages yet to come, long after we too shall have passed away, a saved and grateful republic will rear in history and everlasting memorial to their devotion and their valor, more changeless than brass and more enduring than marble, and that shall exist as long as these voiceless hills bear testimony to Gettysburg's fateful days; and among the immortal names preserved as those the nation delights to honor in all the future, a high and honored place shall be forever held by the old Eleventh Pennsylvania Volunteers...

"And now, to the memory of our fallen companion of the old Eleventh Pennsylvania Volunteers, the heroic dead who lost their lives in the service of their country, and to the regiment in whose ranks they fell, this monument is solemnly dedicated by their surviving comrades. May its silent presence teach more eloquently than language can express, the lessons of patriotism and self-sacrificing devotion to country."

The 11th Pennsylvania monument can be found northwest of Gettysburg on the west side of Doubleday Avenue about 280 yards south of Mummasburg Road.

Acknowledgements

I am extremely grateful for the following people who have supported and encouraged me with this book.

To my family. Thank you for your support of my writing and love of history. Thank you for encouraging me, pushing me along when I wanted to give up, and listening to my moments of panic over this book. I couldn't have done this without you. Mom, thank you for spending hours going over all the edits with me. I love you all!

A huge thank you goes to Emily Chapman, my writing buddy. Thank you for your edits and suggestions, and also for your encouraging words such as, "I love your book!" and "Can I please marry Joe?" You make me smile!

I'm so thankful for my sister-in-law, Maria Putzke. Thank you for your edits and excitement over *It Took a War*. I'm blessed to call you my sister!

To one of my best friends, Michaela Richmond. Thank you for showing me how to be a Civil War reenactor, which played a big part in writing this book! Thank you for checking historical accuracy and details. I can't thank you enough, Mike!

Thank you to Betty Lundberg, for your encouragement through this publishing process and my writing. You inspire me with your own love of writing!

To Grandma Farnand for passing on your love of reading, and to Grandpa Farnand whose stories are one of a kind! I hope to someday be as good of a storyteller as you!

Rachel Rossano, thank you for the beautiful cover and formatting. You are so wonderful to work with!

You would not be holding this book in your hands were it not for this group of amazing people.

"Glory be to Him whose power, working in us, can do infinitely more than we can ask or imagine; glory be to Him from generation to generation in the Church and in Christ Jesus for ever and ever. Amen."
– Ephesians 3: 14-21

Bibliography

Books:

Abraham, Donna J. *The Way They Were Dressed in 1860-1865*. Abraham's Lady, LLC, 2011

Arnold, James R, and Wiener, Roberta. *Life Goes On: The Civil War at Home*. Lerner Pub Group (L), 2001

Billings, John D. *Hardtack and Coffee*. Bison Books; Reprint edition, 1993

Damon, Duane. *Growing Up in the Civil War*. Lerner Pub Group (L), 2002

Graham, Martin F. *A Pocket History of the Civil War*. Osprey Publishing, 2011

Leisch, Juanita. *An Introduction to Civil War Civilians*. Thomas Publications; First edition, 1994

Miller, William J. *The Training of an Army: Camp Curtin and the North's Civil War*. White Mane Publishing Company; First Edition, 1990

Murphy, Jim. *The Boys War*. HMH Books for Young Readers; Reissue edition, 1993

Wiley, Bell I. *The Life of Billy Yank*. Louisiana State Univ Pr; Updated edition, 2008

Zucchero, Michael. *Loyal Hearts (Histories of American Civil War Canines)* Schroeder Publications; 2nd edition, 2009

Websites:

"A Much-Needed Simplified Introduction to Civil War Drill."
http://www.4catstudio.com/chickamauga/CW%20drill%20-%20simplified%20Rev.%20B.pdf

Bates, Samuel P. "History of Pennsylvania volunteers, 1861-5; prepared in compliance with acts of the legislature."
http://quod.lib.umich.edu/m/moa/ABY3439.0001.001/124?rgn=full+text;view=image

Blakeslee, Bob. "Sallie, Mascot of the 11th PA Volunteer Infantry." 2002 - 2014,
http://www.nycivilwar.us/sallie.html

Bemis, Todd. "Civil War Bugle Calls." 2012,
http://civilwarbuglecalls.blogspot.com/

Gayley, Alice J. "11th Regiment Pennsylvania Volunteers."
http://www.pa-roots.com/pacw/infantry/11th/11thorg.html

Gayley, Alice J. "11th Regiment Pennsylvania Volunteers 3-Years Service Company I."
http://www.pa-roots.com/pacw/infantry/11th/11thcoi3yr.html

Gayley, Alice J. "Pennsylvania in the Civil War."
http://www.pa-roots.com/pacw/infantry/paregimentsnew1.html

Hawks, Steve A. "11th PA Volunteer Infantry Regiment." 2007-2014,
http://www.gettysburg.stonesentinels.com/PA/11Pa.php

openlibrary.org "Pennsylvania at Gettysburg."

https://archive.org/stream/pennsylvania02penn___pa
ge/n197/mode/2up

Pennsylvania Civil War Volunteers."PA Civil War
Volunteer Soldiers." 1997-2013,
http://www.pacivilwar.com/regiment/11th.html

"PA Civil War Battle Flags." PA Capitol Preservation
Committee,
http://www.pacivilwarflags.org/regiments/indivFlag.cfm?
accsn=1985.009

Sheil, T and Sheil, A. "Civil War Drill from Casey's
Tactics, 1862." 2006,
http://www.thortrains.com/getright/drillcasey1.htm

Shenandoah Valley History Center. "Tour of the Civil
War in the Shenandoah Valley."
http://www.angelfire.com/va3/valleywar/0tour_martinsb
urg.htm

Videos:

Civil War Trust. "Battle of Gettysburg Animated Map."
2012,
http://www.civilwar.org/battlefields/gettysburg/maps/ge
ttysburg-animated-map/

"Loading and Firing a Civil War Rifled Musket."
https://www.youtube.com/watch?v=B9mSwbvz2oE

"9 Steps to Load and Fire a Civil War Rifle."
https://vimeo.com/40840882

About the Author

Emily Ann Putzke is a young novelist, historical reenactor, and history lover. Learn more about Emily and her books at www.authoremilyannputzke.com and amazon.com/author/emilyannputzke.

Facebook:
https://www.facebook.com/authoremilyannputzke
Pinterest:
http://www.pinterest.com/emilyannputzke/
Instagram:
http://instagram.com/authoremilyannputzke/

Made in the USA
Monee, IL
18 July 2022